SpringerBriefs in Political Science

SpringerBriefs present concise summaries of cutting-edge research and practical applications across a wide spectrum of fields. Featuring compact volumes of 50 to 125 pages, the series covers a range of content from professional to academic. Typical topics might include:

- A timely report of state-of-the art analytical techniques
- A bridge between new research results, as published in journal articles, and a contextual literature review
- A snapshot of a hot or emerging topic
- An in-depth case study or clinical example
- A presentation of core concepts that students must understand in order to make independent contributions

SpringerBriefs in Political Science showcase emerging theory, empirical research, and practical application in political science, policy studies, political economy, public administration, political philosophy, international relations, and related fields, from a global author community.

SpringerBriefs are characterized by fast, global electronic dissemination, standard publishing contracts, standardized manuscript preparation and formatting guidelines, and expedited production schedules.

Arno Tausch

Political Islam and Religiously Motivated Political Extremism

An International Comparison

 Springer

Arno Tausch
Department of Political Studies
and Governance
University of the Free State
Bloemfontein, South Africa

This project is funded by the Austrian Fund for the Documentation of Religiously Motivated Political Extremism (Dokumentationsstelle Politischer Islam)

ISSN 2191-5466　　　　　　　　ISSN 2191-5474　(electronic)
SpringerBriefs in Political Science
ISBN 978-3-031-24853-5　　　　ISBN 978-3-031-24854-2　(eBook)
https://doi.org/10.1007/978-3-031-24854-2

© The Author(s) 2023. This book is an open access publication.

Open Access This book is licensed under the terms of the Creative Commons Attribution 4.0 International License (http://creativecommons.org/licenses/by/4.0/), which permits use, sharing, adaptation, distribution and reproduction in any medium or format, as long as you give appropriate credit to the original author(s) and the source, provide a link to the Creative Commons license and indicate if changes were made.

The images or other third party material in this book are included in the book's Creative Commons license, unless indicated otherwise in a credit line to the material. If material is not included in the book's Creative Commons license and your intended use is not permitted by statutory regulation or exceeds the permitted use, you will need to obtain permission directly from the copyright holder.

The use of general descriptive names, registered names, trademarks, service marks, etc. in this publication does not imply, even in the absence of a specific statement, that such names are exempt from the relevant protective laws and regulations and therefore free for general use.

The publisher, the authors, and the editors are safe to assume that the advice and information in this book are believed to be true and accurate at the date of publication. Neither the publisher nor the authors or the editors give a warranty, expressed or implied, with respect to the material contained herein or for any errors or omissions that may have been made. The publisher remains neutral with regard to jurisdictional claims in published maps and institutional affiliations.

This Springer imprint is published by the registered company Springer Nature Switzerland AG
The registered company address is: Gewerbestrasse 11, 6330 Cham, Switzerland

Foreword

Professor Tausch in his outstanding research deals with the different interpretations of what is called "political Islam", its main characteristics and its implications.

Indeed, political Islam is the result of a socio-economic-political phenomenon and certainly not the reflection of yet other terrorist organisations. Most of the analysts have looked at the Islamic State (ISIS) as another terrorist organisation, an Al-Qaeda offshoot, waging a guerrilla war with cohorts of unorganised thugs. The Afghani-style gear, the pickup trucks, the all black or army fatigue uniforms that most ISIS fighters wear, the unshaven beards, the turbans, hoods and head "bandanas" with Arabic inscriptions have added to the confusion.

To understand the political Islam phenomenon, it is crucial to examine the factors that contributed to its emergence:

Since the fall of Muslim empires and supremacy, Muslim scholars and philosophers have tried to understand the reasons behind its collapse, its domination by Western powers, its colonisation and its incapacity to reproduce the genius that so much characterised the Muslim civilisation following the conquests that stretched the Muslim lands from Spain to India, West Asia and China. Most, if not all the scholars tried to analyse the characteristics behind the "Golden Age" of Islam and why at a certain point, the Muslim world stopped producing innovations in science, medicine, algebra, mathematics, military warfare machines and graphic arts. The conclusion of most was that Muslim civilization had drifted away from the teachings of the Koran and adopted foreign and heretical inputs that had destroyed its fabric. The remedy they proposed was to return to the "pure Islam" which would heal the wounds and respond to the West by first reconstructing the Muslim society according to their raw interpretation of the Koran and organising to defeat Western power.

Indeed, since the fall of Muslim Spain in the fifteenth century and especially since the beginning of Western colonisation of Muslim territories, the Muslim world has witnessed the rise and fall of successive radical movements whose prime aim was to combat the West while regenerating the original Muslim society of Prophet Mohammad which was thought to be the cure for all ailments. Muslim thinkers like Jamal ad-Din al-Afghani (late nineteenth century), Muhammad 'Abduh (nineteenth century), Sayyed Qutub (twentieth century), Muhammad Iqbal (early twentieth century) and the Muhammad Ahmad al-Mahdi in Sudan (nineteenth century) are only a few examples of Muslim radicals who inspired upheavals against Western powers.

Since the Soviet intervention in Afghanistan, foreign military intervention in the latter part of the twentieth century, be it Soviet or American, was greatly responsible for the awakening of Sunni radicalism in West and Central Asia and to its expression today as a Holy War against the West, its allies and Israel. The perception that the West led by the USA are the new Crusaders trying to subdue Islam has nurtured extremists ideologies and created many militant organisations whose mission is to fight "the infidels". This perception should be considered to be at the root of the creation of Al-Qaeda whose raison d'être is to fight the West and to strive to re-create a Muslim (Sunni) caliphate in the areas extending from North Africa to "Ma wara al Nahr", meaning Central and Eastern Asia, the historical boundaries of the once Islamic empire.

The civil war in Syria transformed very quickly into a radical Sunni armed insurrection against the Alawite Iranian-backed Assad regime. The Muslim Brotherhood, which led the battle against the regime at the beginning of the conflict, was soon joined by radical organisations financed not only by Saudi Arabia and Qatar but also by other actors such as the USA, UK, France and Turkey. Qatar alone is said to have poured into the conflict more than $500 million. The Syrian scene provided all the ingredients for the radicalisation of Sunni organisations. The Syrian civil war is an "all-in-one" situation in which all the previous factors are involved: foreign presence, Sunnis against Shiites, Iran and Hizbullah, Saudi Arabia and Qatar, the USA, France and Turkey and an international coalition led by the USA fighting Islamic militants in the lands of Islam.

Saudi Arabia and Qatar fund Islamic organisations all over the world, nurturing mainly the Salafi-Wahhabi schools at the expense of traditional and moderate Islam. Most of the Muslim states have been exposed for a long time to Wahhabi proselytism that is by essence opposed to the "moderate" Sufi Islam practised in North Africa. No wonder after the revolution in Libya and the takeover of Mali by Islamic fundamentalists, the Muslim militants destroyed all religious shrines, an exact copy of the reality in Saudi Arabia and Qatar.

The Islamic Republic of Iran has also played a major catalyst role in contributing to the polarisation of the Muslim world into two rival camps, Shiites and Sunnites. Since the beginning of the Khomeini takeover in 1979, Iran has been preaching a pan-Islamist ideology while sealing alliances with Islamic movements in the Arab world, Africa and Asia. Iran concealed its Shiite philosophy and succeeded in creating the illusion that it was transcending its origins and its identity as a Shiite entity. It was not until the beginning of the so-called Arab Spring that the Arab nations realised the Iranian scheme. The war in Syria and Iran's open alliance with the Assad regime and the Shiite regime in Baghdad, Iran's subversive activity in Lebanon through Hizbullah and the Houthis in Yemen, unveiled the implications of the Iranian contribution: the transformation of local conflicts in West Asia into a Shiite-Sunni open conflict over hegemony. Moreover, the Arab perception that the US administration was looking to mend the fences with Iran at the expense of its historical clients in the Middle East accelerated the crisis between the Arab world and Iran and justified in the eyes of many the armed struggle waged by the Islamists against Iran and its allies in the region.

Another factor in the rise of political Islam is the so-called Arab Spring which was the expression of the failure of the Arab nation states. The events in Egypt, Tunisia, Syria, Bahrain and Yemen were exploited by Islamic militant movements which found the right opportunity to rise from their clandestine activities after years of oppression and persecution by the different Arab regimes to the forefront of the political struggle for power. Years of military rule did not eradicate the Islamic political forces that had remained in the shadow and camouflaged themselves under the cover of charitable organisations, social assistance and non-profit entities. However, after a first round in which the Islamists seemingly won in Tunisia and Egypt, the secular forces backed by the military succeeded in overcoming the Islamists. The Muslim Brotherhood was dealt a heavy blow both in Syria and Egypt. However, the different regimes were unsuccessful in eradicating the plethora of militant terrorist Islamic organisations that are still conducting their deadly attacks against the different regimes. Some regimes survived—even though deeply shaken and destabilised— like Egypt, Tunisia, Algeria and Morocco—while others like Libya deteriorated into failed states, and others are struggling for their survival such as Syria, Lebanon, Iraq and Yemen.

The second American war in Iraq in 2003 dealt a death blow to the Sunni minority that had ruled Iraq since its separation from the Ottoman Empire by British colonialism. The Americans, striving to establish a new "world order" with democratic regimes as a copy of the West, established an unprecedented Shiite regime which in turn discriminated against the Sunnites who found themselves out of jobs, positions, army command and Baath party offices. Paul Bremer, then Head of the US occupational authority in Baghdad, disbanded the Iraqi army in May 2003. Thousands of well-trained Sunni officers were robbed of their livelihood with the stroke of a pen. In doing so, America created its most bitter and intelligent enemies.

Never in the modern history of the Muslim world has a conflict drawn so many jihadists as is the case with the Syrian and Iraqi civil wars, surpassing wars in Afghanistan in 2001 and Iraq in 2003. Syria and Iraq have become the epicentre of the global Jihad.

The jihadists who are the militant expression of political Islam seek to participate in the establishment of an Islamic Caliphate to rule the world after the defeat in battle of the Western powers and their local Arab allies. The attraction exercised on Sunni Muslims around the globe and in the Arab and Muslim world is tremendous.

The attraction is not limited in space or time. The movement is in Europe, the USA, Australia, Xinyang and also in the Arab world and Africa. As a matter of fact, most of North Africa's jihadist groups were hesitant to associate themselves with the Islamic State until the USA commenced its military intervention in Iraq and Syria in August 2014.

Religion does not have much to do with political Islam. Most Jihadists know nothing about Islam and mindlessly repeat some verses that have been hammered into them by radical imams, less stupid than them, but much more dangerous. Those who are outside these profiles are only a tiny minority—exceptions that confirm the rule. Jihadist university graduates, for instance, are often frustrated individuals who have failed to integrate into society through work, study, socialisation, marriage, etc. There again, radical imams succeed to convince them that their failures are not of their making but that of the environment that dismisses them. They teach them the idea that it is legitimate that they restore the situation to their benefit and by acting with force.

In fact, political Islam has transformed into a psychiatric pathology, characteristics of obsessive-compulsive, even depressive disorders, as well as an inability to be socialised.

As such the study conducted by Prof. Tausch is of the utmost importance in order to understand the expressions of political Islam.

Jerusalem, Israel
Colonel (Ret.) Dr. Jacques Neriah
Former Head of Assessment at Israel's
Directorate of Military intelligence
Senior Researcher at the Jerusalem
Center for Public Affairs
Senior Security Commentator on
i24news TV channels

Preface

This study was financed by the Austrian "*Dokumentationsstelle Politischer Islam*" and attempts an analysis of what can be said about the phenomenon of "*political Islam*" in the Arab world and what can be said about religiously motivated political extremism (hereafter abbreviated RMPE) in an international comparison from the perspective of international, empirically oriented social sciences. We use open, internationally accessible data from the *Arab Barometer* and the *World Values Survey* to analyse these two phenomena.

The study shows that there is a very broad consensus in research in the leading *peer-reviewed journals* of the social sciences and in the publications of the world's leading book publishers to work with the concept of "*political Islam*", whereby this analytical-conceptual consensus also includes those who, such as former US President Barack Obama, in his famous *Presidential Study Directive No 11,* even see an opportunity for cooperation with *political Islam,* which rejects terrorism, or the French sociologist Francois Burgat, who aggressively argues for an alliance of *political Islam* with the political left of the West. Important research figures in international Middle East studies, such as the aforementioned Francois Burgat, but also Jocelyne Cesari, John Esposito, Gilles Kepel, Oliver Roy, all of them, and for all the differences they may have in their approach to the phenomenon, have all written important texts on *political Islam* with this term in the title of their studies, and the author of the present study finds it untenable when today, for example, the Federal Agency for Civic Education (Bundeszentrale für politische Bildung), which is subordinate to the German Ministry of the Interior, writes that whoever uses this term is engaging in "alarmist thinking, placing Muslims under a "general suspicion", fishing in the right-wing pond of voters, and using a term that has incitement potential". This view, expressed by the Federal Agency for Civic Education in Bonn in the language that is so common in Europe today and that covers large sections of the academic community and the opinion columns of the major daily newspapers seems to be becoming more and more popular.

The author of this study counters this view with the fact that outstanding Arab researchers who teach at Princeton, New Jersey; Amman, Jordan; and Qatar University in Qatar, such as Amaney Jamal,[1] Darwish Al-Emadi[2] and Musa Shteiwi,[3] as senior researchers of the *"Arab Barometer"* project, explicitly use the term *"political Islam"* in their questionnaire with five interview items. The extension of the term *"political Islam"* is practically undisputed. In the mathematical logic and analytical philosophy of the Vienna Circle by Rudolf Carnap (1891–1970), there is a tradition of relying on the extension of a contested term when debating a phenomenon over whose conceptual meaning there is such polarisation. In our case—of *"political Islam"*—the research of the Arab Barometer as well as Francois Burgat, but also Jocelyne Cesari, John Esposito, Gilles Kepel and Oliver Roy clearly outlines which important value patterns the adherents of *political Islam* represent (five items from the Arab Barometer) and which political movements and governments of countries are to be assigned to the extension of the phenomenon, such as the Muslim Brotherhood in Egypt, Sudan and Jordan, Jamaat-i-Islami in South Asia, the Refah Party in Turkey, the Islamic Salvation Front in Algeria, al Nahda in Tunisia, Hizballah in Lebanon, Hamas and Islamic Jihad in the Palestinian territories and Gamaa Islamiyya and Jihad in Egypt. Instead of relying on sheer endless debates about "correct" and "permissible" and "incorrect" and "to be avoided" terms (German-speaking intellectuals are particularly fond of such useless debates), let us ask ourselves radically: if it is clear anyway who and what is meant by *"political Islam"*, let us instead look very closely at the empirical phenomena that characterise the adherents of *"political Islam"* and what relations exist with other empirically ascertainable phenomena.

In the light of the literature mentioned, it is certainly also legitimate to describe the current AKP government in Turkey and the Islamist regime in Iran as *"political Islam in power"*. Our measurement of *"political Islam"* adopts the perspective outlined here 1:1. After all, according to the *"Arab Barometer"* team, *"political Islam"* occurs whenever the following opinions are held in the region:

- It is better for religious leaders to hold public office
- Religious leaders should influence government decisions
- Religious leaders are less corrupt than civilian ones
- Religious leaders should influence elections
- Religious practice is not a private matter.

The empirical-analytical starting point for our analyses is then an important study by Harvard Professor Melanie Cammett (Cammett et al., 2020), which deals explicitly with *political Islam* and political values in the Arab world using data from the *Arab Barometer*. The empirical analyses of Cammett et al., 2020, use longitudinal data from the Arab Barometer as well as data from the *World Values Survey* 2015.

---

[1] https://scholar.google.com/citations?hl=en&user=CqNmnVwAAAAJ&view_op=list_works. All downloads of this study were re-checked by 12 May 2022.
[2] https://scholar.google.com/scholar?hl=en&as_sdt=0%2C5&q=Darwish+Al-Emadi+&btnG=.
[3] https://scholar.google.com/citations?hl=en&user=jw3SvkQAAAAJ.

After presenting the most important existing studies on the topic, the author then goes into the methodological prerequisites of our empirical study and discusses the data sets, the statistical methods and also the ranges of variation in the results.

The empirical analyses based on IBM-SPSS-24 promax factor analyses of 24 variables according to the *Arab Barometer* explicitly measure *political Islam* with five variables and also determine the environment (19 variables) of *political Islam* and its consequences, such as the lack of tolerance towards other religions, identification with states that today clearly represent *political Islam,* such as the regime in Iran, President Erdogan in Turkey, restrictive gender norms as defined by the UNDP Human Development Report, 2019, the belief that Muslims should enjoy greater rights in a state than non-Muslims, the negative fixation against the USA, UK and Israel in world politics, the call for a *Sharia* that explicitly introduces corporal punishment and restricts women's rights and expressing a sympathetic understanding of acts of anti-American terror in the Middle East.

The Arab Barometer asks the populations in the Arab world about the countries with which the "*Arab publics*" in the region identify very strongly. The study clearly shows that identification with Turkey and Iran, with a *political Islam* that also influences elections and results in a theocracy, promotes religious and gender discrimination and advocates an Islamist interpretation of Islam, is very much the most important, interrelated syndromes of *political Islam*, which together explain more than 50% of the total variance of the 24 model variables used. Therefore, in the final analysis, our study is highly sceptical of such approaches as the aforementioned perspective of President Obama and his *presidential study directive No. 11* and forms a further argument in favour of the orientation used as a basis in the study, as expressed in the "*Strategic Survey for Israel 2019*" by the Institute for National Security Studies in Tel Aviv, Israel (INSS, 2020). If the states of Europe want to win the fight against jihadism, they must work closely with the moderate Arab states, such as Egypt, Jordan, Morocco, Saudi Arabia, the United Arab Emirates and other Arab Gulf states, and be aware that, on a population-weighted basis, 41% of all Arabs now view the Muslim Brotherhood, which is the strongest and most coherent force in *political Islam* today, negatively or very negatively. According to the data brought to light here, only 7% of people in the Arab world now have a high level of trust in their country's Islamist movement, while 14% have some trust, 19% have little trust, but 60% have no trust. It is also time for the current ruling political elites in Washington D.C. to face up to these realities and correct the fundamental mistakes made in this regard during the Obama era. This is also the reason why the author of this study came to such a positive conclusion about the so-called Abraham treaties in a recent publication in the Gulf states. Our overall index—Overcoming Political Islam—shows that Morocco and Tunisia are the top performers, while Iraq and Sudan bring up the rear. Following an important study by Falco and Rotondi, 2016, we also explore the question of whether political Islam is more prevalent or less prevalent among the more than 20% of the Arab population who plan to emigrate in the coming years than among the population as a whole. Far from feeding alarmist horror scenarios, our evaluation shows firstly that Falco and Rotondi, 2016, are correct in their thesis that among potential migrants to the West, *political Islam is* certainly less pronounced than among the Arab population as a whole. On a population-weighted basis, only 13.11% of potential migrants to the West openly state that they trust the country-specific Islamist movement.

In the second part of our empirical evaluations, we explore religiously motivated political extremism (RMPE) by international comparison on the basis of the following items of the *World Values Survey*, which are sparse but nevertheless available on this topic:

- Many things are desirable, but not all of them are necessary components of a democracy. For each of the following things, please tell me to what extent you consider it to be a necessary component of a democracy. Use this scale, where 1 stands for "not at all a necessary part of a democracy" and 10 for "a necessary part of a democracy". **Religious leaders ultimately determine the interpretation of laws.**
- For each of the following points, can you please tell me whether you think this is okay under no circumstances, **okay under any circumstances,** or anything in between? Please use the following scale. **Politically motivated violence.**

It is strongly recommended that our results are used with due care and awareness of the statistical margins of error that are detailed in our analysis.

The most important further results are the following: the proportion of people who favour religious authorities in interpreting the law while accepting political violence is alarmingly high in various parts of the world, raising fears of numerous conflicts in the coming years in an increasingly unstable world system. It amounts to more than half of the adult population in Tajikistan (the international record holder) and Malaysia and some non-Muslim-majority countries. In many countries, including NATO and EU member states, it is an alarming 25–50%, and we mention here the Muslim-majority countries Iraq, Lebanon, Bangladesh, Kazakhstan, Nigeria and Indonesia. It is 15–25% even in core countries of the Western security architecture, but also in the Muslim-majority countries: Pakistan, Iran and Tunisia. Only in the best-ranked countries, among them the Muslim-majority countries Albania, Egypt, Bosnia and Herzegovina, Kyrgyzstan, Azerbaijan and Jordan, the potentially fatal combination of mixing religion and law and accepting political violence has a relatively small following of less than 15%.

In the sense of the theses of the late Harvard economist Alberto Alesina (1957–2020), social trust is an essential general production factor of any social order, and the institutions of national security of the democratic West would do well to make good use of this capital of trust that also exists among Muslims living in the West.

Bloemfontein, South Africa   Arno Tausch

Contents

1 Introduction: What This Study Is Not and What It Aspires to Be 1
2 *"Political Islam"*—A Contested Term 7
   2.1 The Scientific GPS for the Analysis of Politics in the Middle East 9
   2.2 Political Islam 11
   2.3 "Political Islam" and Its Open Supporters 13
      2.3.1 Political Islam—Not a Gateway Drug to Islamist Terror (Hashemi Study, 2021) 14
      2.3.2 For an Explicit Alliance of the Global Left and Political Islam: Francois Burgat (2019) 16
3 The Scientific Background to Our Own Empirical Study 19
   3.1 Political Islam: The Information Potential of Fox's et al. (2016) and Achilov's (2016) Studies on Political Islam Based on the Arab Barometer 20
   3.2 The Studies by Falco and Rotondi 21
   3.3 The Studies Whose Design Was Important for Our Own Empirical Investigation 22
      3.3.1 The Cammett et al. (2020) Study 22
      3.3.2 The Cesari Study, 2021 23
      3.3.3 The Driessen (2018) Study 25
      3.3.4 The Kucinskas and Van Der Does (2017) Study 25
      3.3.5 The Rahbarqazi and Mahmoudoghli (2020) Study 27
      3.3.6 The Tessler (2010), Study 29
4 Methods and Design of Our Own Empirical Study 33
   4.1 The Survey-Based Methodology in Comparative Social Research and the Potential of the World Values Survey 34
   4.2 The Design of the Study 36
   4.3 The Quantitative-Statistical Methodology 39
   4.4 The Multivariate Methods 40

4.5	The Error Margins	41
4.6	Traceability	41
	4.6.1 Arab Barometer	42
	4.6.2 The Files of the World Values Survey	43
4.7	Macro-quantitative Country Data	43

5 The Empirical Results of Our Empirical Study 45
   5.1 Results on Political Islam According to the Arab Barometer 46
   5.2 Political Islam and Migration Potential According to the Arab
        Barometer 52
   5.3 Towards a Multivariate Analysis of Political Islam and Migration ... 56
       5.3.1 Conclusions and Perspectives from the Arab Barometer
             Data 56
   5.4 Results of the World Values Survey on Religiously Motivated
        Political Extremism (RMPE) in Europe Compared to 79
        Countries in the World 57
       5.4.1 The Multivariate Results of the World Values Survey
             on Religiously Motivated Political Extremism (RMPE) 62
       5.4.2 The Extent and Global Drivers of Acceptance of Political
             Violence and Religiously Motivated Political Extremism
             (RMPE)—Multivariate Analysis of World Values
             Survey Data at the Global Level 65

**6 Discussion and Conclusions of This Study in the Context
of the Empirical Results Obtained** 77
   6.1 Political Islam and Terrorism 78
   6.2 Open Society and Political Islam 79
   6.3 For an Integration Policy Based on Trust in the Spirit of Harvard
        Professor Alberto Alesina (1957–2020) 80

Literature Used and Further Reading 83

About the Author

Arno Tausch was born on 11 February 1951 in Salzburg, Austria. He is currently Visiting Professor of Political Studies and Governance, University of the Free State, Bloemfontein, South Africa (as of 1 May 2022) and was Honorary Associate Professor of Economics, Corvinus University, Budapest, Hungary (since Fall Semester 2010). He is also Adjunct Professor (Universitaetsdozent) of Political Science at Innsbruck University, Department of Political Science, Innsbruck University, Austria (since 1988).

He entered the Austrian Civil Service on 1 January 1992 and retired from active service on 29 February 2016. He served as an Austrian diplomat abroad and was Attaché, and later Counselor for Labor and Migration at the Austrian Embassy in Warsaw, 1992–1999. In that capacity, he was deeply involved in the democratic transformation of Poland and in the assessment of all major social and migration policy aspects of the Polish accession to the European Union with Polish partner institutions. He also closely worked with his fellow labour and migration attaches from other Western countries in Warsaw, in particular the representatives of the Delegation of the European Commission and the Embassies of France, Germany, the USA, and the United Nations Development Programme and the UNHCR in Warsaw.

In his multiple academic assignments, stretching over a time span of four decades, he was first Assistant Professor and then Associate Professor in the Department of Political Science at Innsbruck University; Associate Visiting Professor of Political Science at the University of Hawaii at Manoa, 1990, and Guest Researcher, International Institute for Comparative Social Research, Science Center, West Berlin, upon invitation by the late Karl Wolfgang Deutsch, Stanfield Professor of International Peace at Harvard University (1981). Since 1978, he taught numerous regular courses in political science, economics and sociology at universities in Austria, Hungary, Switzerland and in the USA.

He authored or co-authored books and articles for major international publishers and journals, among them 25 books in English, 2 books in French, 8 books in German, and currently 116 articles in peer-reviewed journals, 31 articles in collective volumes and also numerous press articles in the media of several countries. In all, his works were published or re-published in 33 countries around the globe.

His publications also include a number of essays for leading economic and foreign policy global think tanks like the

- Austrian Institute for International Affairs, Vienna (ÖIIP);
- Austrian National Defence Academy (Vienna), LAVAK;
- Center for Security Studies, CSS, ETH Zurich;
- Centre Franco-Autrichien pour le rapprochement en Europe CFA/OeFZ, Vienne;
- Centro Argentino de Estudios Internacionales, CAEI, Buenos Aires;
- Hoover Institution, Stanford, California;
- Insight Turkey, Ankara;
- Institute for National Security Studies (INSS), Tel Aviv, Israel;
- Institute of World Economy and International Relations (IMEMO RAS Institute), Moscow;
- IZA Institute of Labour Economics (Bonn);
- Jean Monnet Chairs of the European Union https://eacea.ec.europa.eu/erasmus-plus/actions/jean-monnet/jean-monnet-chairs_en (Jean Monnet Chairs at the University of Catania, Sicily; Italy, Trier, FRG; and Wroclaw, Poland);
- Jerusalem Center for Public Affairs (JCPA), Jerusalem, Israel;
- Luxembourg Institute for European and International Studies, LIEIS;
- Polish Institute for International Affairs PISM, Warsaw;
- Rubin Center in International Affairs (formerly Global Research in International Affairs (GLORIA) Center) in Herzliya, Israel;
- Vienna Institute for International Economic Studies, WIIW.

His publications feature(d) as recommended materials for courses at major Universities and centres of higher learning around the world, including the School of International Service, American University, Washington D.C.; and Harvard University, and were referred to in publications by the European Trade Union Institute, the IMF, the OECD, the World Bank, and the United Nations Development Programme (UNDP).

Major electronic English language publications are freely accessible from the World Systems Archive at the University of California, Riverside; from IDEAS/REPEC at the University of Connecticut; and from SSRN, the Social Science Research Network in New York, N.Y. Dr. Tausch, a liberal and active Roman Catholic, is a participant in the liberation theology movement and in the ecumenical dialogue between the major world religions since the 1970s.

List of Figures

Fig. 4.1	Maximum geographical coverage of the *World Values Survey* in wave 4 (2010–2014) and wave 5 (2017–2020) for multivariate analysis. *Source* Our own SPSS calculations from the data of the *World Values Survey*, https://www.worldvaluessurvey.org/WVSContents.jsp	34
Fig. 4.2	"*Political Islam*" in our *Arab Barometer* IBM-SPSS Data File	37
Fig. 5.1	Acceptance of political violence	60
Fig. 5.2	Religious authorities should interpret the laws	61
Fig. 6.1	Sharia with corporal punishment in Europe? The Herculean task of changing values in the Arab world—population-weighted shares of the total Arab population that clearly support Islamist positions according to the Arab *Barometer* data	80

List of Tables

Table 4.1	Maximum ranges of variation for survey results (the probability of error is 5%)	42
Table 5.1	Trust in Islamist movements in the Arab world	47
Table 5.2	Islamism and *political Islam* in the Arab MENA countries	48
Table 5.3	*Political Islam* among those willing to migrate and in the Arab population as a whole according to the Arab *Barometer*	49
Table 5.4	*Political Islam* in the Arab world according to the *Arab Barometer* (only valid percentages were evaluated)	50
Table 5.5	Desire to emigrate to Western countries, in % of the total Arab population according to the Arab *Barometer*	53
Table 5.6	Trust in the Islamist movement of the respective home country as a percentage of the total Arab population and as a percentage of the Arab population willing to emigrate to the West	54
Table 5.7	Support for *political Islam* (five items according to the Arab Barometer survey) as a percentage of the total Arab population willing to emigrate to the West and as a percentage of the total Arab population	55
Table 5.8	Parametric index: overcoming *Political Islam*	66
Table 5.9	Parametric index: overcoming *political Islam* for those wanting to emigrate in the Arab world to the West	66
Table 5.10	RMPE in Austria according to the *World Values Survey*	66
Table 5.11	RMPE at international level according to the *World Values Survey*	67
Table 5.12	Regression-analytical model of the drivers of acceptance of political violence—multivariate analysis of *World Values Survey* data at the global level	70

Table 5.13	Partial correlation of factors influencing acceptance of political violence—multivariate analysis of *World Values Survey* data at the global level (constant: HDI 2018 & (HDI 2018)^2)	72
Table 5.14	Regression-analytical model of the drivers of acceptance of religiously motivated political extremism—multivariate analysis of *World Values Survey* data at the global level	74

List of Electronic Appendix Charts

https://www.academia.edu/79716351/Electronic_Appendix_Political_Islam_and_Religiously_Motivated_Political_Extremism_An_International_Comparison

Electronic Appendix Figure 1	Maximum range of variation for small samples. The probability of error is 5%
Electronic Appendix Figure 2	Standard deviation—acceptance of political violence
Electronic Appendix Figure 3	The depth of the problem that residents of a country endorse political violence
Electronic Appendix Figure 4	% Accept political violence + Interpretation of laws by religious authorities
Electronic Appendix Figure 5	The Depth of the Problem of Inhabitants of a Country Endorsing political violence + Interpretation of Laws by Religious Authorities
Electronic Appendix Figure 6	Radicalisation of the anti-Kelsen camp (% of the population who want religious authorities to interpret the laws endorse political violence)
Electronic Appendix Figure 7	Residuals of our multiple regression analysis on the drivers of acceptance of political violence according to World Values Survey
Electronic Appendix Figure 8	Residuals of our multiple regression equation on the drivers of religiously motivated political extremism, worldwide

List of Electronic Appendix Tables

https://www.academia.edu/79716351/Electronic_Appendix_Political_Islam_and_Religiously_Motivated_Political_Extremism_An_International_Comparison

Electronic Appendix Table 1	Trust in Islamist movements in the Arab world
Electronic Appendix Table 2	Support for political Islam (five items according to the Arab Barometer survey) as a percentage of the total Arab population willing to emigrate to the West and as a percentage of the total Arab population
Electronic Appendix Table 3	Islamist terrorism, political Islam and migration in Western Europe. Eigenvalues of the Promax Factor Analysis
Electronic Appendix Table 4	Factor Loadings—Political Islam
Electronic Appendix Table 5	Component correlations—Political Islam
Electronic Appendix Table 6	Parametric Index: Overcoming "Political Islam"
Electronic Appendix Table 7	Desired migration destinations and "Political Islam"
Electronic Appendix Table 8	Factor analytical model with the RMPE World Values Survey data—Eigenvalues and explained variance
Electronic Appendix Table 9	Factor-analytical model with the RMPE World Values Survey data (Promax factor analysis)—factor loadings
Electronic Appendix Table 10	Factor-analytical model with the data of the World Values Survey (promax factor analysis) of the RMPE—correlation matrix of the components
Electronic Appendix Table 11	Factor analytical model with the RMPE's World Values Survey data (Promax factor analysis)—factor scores on a country basis
Electronic Appendix Table 12	Predicted RMPE, actual values RMPE, residuals, based on the regression analytical model of the drivers of religiously motivated political extremism—multivariate analysis of World Values Survey data at the global level

Electronic Appendix Table 13	Informed guesses about the future northward migration of political Islam to France and Germany, calculated using data from Table 6 and Table 8)
Electronic Appendix Table 14	Average Muslim trust in institutions of security in Austria compared to other social groups according to the World Values Survey
Electronic Appendix Table 15	Average trust of Muslims in institutions of international order compared to other social groups according to the World Values Survey
Electronic Appendix Table 16	Average Muslim trust in churches, press, trade unions, parliament, administration, government, parties and ecology movement in Austria compared to other social groups according to the World Values Survey

Chapter 1
Introduction: What This Study Is Not and What It Aspires to Be

Abstract This study, financed by the Austrian "Dokumentationsstelle Politischer Islam", attempts an analysis of what can be said about the phenomenon of "political Islam" in the Arab world and what can be said about religiously motivated political extremism (hereafter abbreviated RMPE) in an international comparison from the perspective of international, empirically oriented social sciences. We use open, internationally accessible data from the Arab Barometer and the World Values Survey to analyse these two phenomena. In this chapter, we describe the general outline of our study. We emphasise that we follow the example of Cammett et al. (2020), in attempting to present our own empirical data from recognised social science surveys on political Islam. In doing so, the focus is on a tradition influenced by the mathematical logic and analytical philosophy of the Vienna Circle through Rudolf Carnap (1988), of relying on the extension of a contested concept. In our case—of "political Islam"—the research of the Arab Barometer as well as Francois Burgat, but also Jocelyne Cesari, John Esposito, Gilles Kepel and Oliver Roy have in any case very clearly outlined which important value patterns the adherents of political Islam represent (five items from the Arab Barometer) and which political movements and governments of countries can be assigned to the extension of the phenomenon, such as the Muslim Brotherhood in Egypt, Sudan and Jordan, Jamaat-i-Islami in South Asia, the Refah Party in Turkey, the Islamic Salvation Front in Algeria, al Nahda in Tunisia, Hizballah in Lebanon, Hamas and Islamic Jihad in the Palestinian territories and Gamaa Islamiyya and Jihad in Egypt. It is certainly also legitimate, in the light of the above literature, to describe the current AKP government in Turkey and the Islamist regime in Iran as "political Islam in power". Our measurement of "political Islam" thus adopts this perspective without "ifs" and "buts" and 1:1. After all, according to the "Arab Barometer" team, "political Islam" occurs whenever the following opinions are held in the region:

- It is better for religious leaders to hold public office
- Religious leaders should influence government decisions
- Religious leaders are less corrupt than civilian ones
- Religious leaders should influence elections
- Religious practice is not a private matter.

Keywords Political Islam · Religiously motivated political extremism · Arab Barometer · World Values Survey · Opinion surveys in the Arab world

The author of this study accepted with interest the invitation of the Austrian *"Dokumentationsstelle Politischer Islam"* to write an analysis of what can be said about the phenomenon of *"political Islam"* in the Arab world and what can be said about religiously motivated political extremism (hereafter abbreviated RMPE) in an international comparison from the perspective of international, empirically oriented social sciences. Such a study by a quantitative political scientist should be conducive to an objectified debate and be useful for all concerned.

This work is by no means a study of *"Islam in Europe"* "per se". Whoever wants to read such an analysis into this publication is mistaken. There are already enough good presentations and analyses of *"Islam"* in Europe in international and also European social science, for example on the website *Euroislam* run by Jocelyn Cesari.[1] Incidentally, the same researcher, Jocelyn Cesari, wrote a study in 2018 on the topic of *"political Islam"* (Cesari, 2018) on a global level.[2]

In this publication, after discussing the conceptual issues, the author, following the example of Cammett et al. (2020), attempts to present his own empirical data from recognised social science surveys on *political Islam*. In doing so, the focus is on a tradition influenced by the mathematical logic and analytical philosophy of the Vienna Circle through Rudolf Carnap (1988), of relying on the extension of a contested concept. In our case—of *"political Islam"*—the research of the *Arab Barometer as* well as Francois Burgat, but also Jocelyne Cesari, John Esposito, Gilles Kepel and Oliver Roy has in any case very clearly outlined which important value patterns the adherents of *political Islam* represent (five items from the Arab Barometer) and which political movements and governments of countries can be assigned to the extension of the phenomenon, such as the Muslim Brotherhood in Egypt, Sudan and Jordan, Jamaat-i-Islami in South Asia, the Refah Party in Turkey, the Islamic Salvation Front in Algeria, al Nahda in Tunisia, Hizballah in Lebanon, Hamas and Islamic Jihad in the Palestinian territories and Gamaa Islamiyya and Jihad in Egypt. It is certainly also legitimate, in the light of the above literature, to describe the current AKP government in Turkey and the Islamist regime in Iran as *"political Islam in power"*. Our measurement of *"political Islam"* thus adopts this perspective without "ifs" and "buts" and 1:1. After all, according to the *"Arab Barometer"* team, *"political Islam"* occurs whenever the following opinions are held in the region:

- It is better for religious leaders to hold public office
- Religious leaders should influence government decisions
- Religious leaders are less corrupt than civilian ones
- Religious leaders should influence elections
- Religious practice is not a private matter.

---

[1] Her website from Harvard Divinity School can be found at https://hds.harvard.edu/people/jocelyne-cesari. The website Euro-Islam can be found at http://www.euro-islam.info/. There are also country dossiers on Islam in Europe http://www.euro-islam.info/country-profiles/.

[2] https://kopfumkrone.at/kultur/farid-hafez-der-politische-islam-ist-tot.

The empirical-analytical starting point for our analyses is thus the important study by Harvard Professor Melanie Cammett (Cammett et al., 2020), which also deals explicitly with *political Islam* and political values in the Arab world using data from the Arab *Barometer.* The empirical analyses by Cammett et al. (2020), use longitudinal data from the Arab Barometer as well as data from the *World Values Survey* 2015.

Although the individual studies reviewed here diverge in details, they all agree that organisations such as the Muslim Brotherhood and Hamas can rightly be described as *"political Islam"*.

The data used here and also the statistical methods are internationally comprehensible, the data are freely available, and the statistical software package IBM-SPSS is implemented at most institutions of tertiary education in the world. Even critics of our publication should come to the same conclusions as those presented here. In debating our findings, it should be noted that the data and perspectives presented here are based on what leading minds in international and Arab political science, including those at educational institutions in Qatar, have come up with about *political Islam. The* same is true of the debate out in the Western world: what is needed is a fact-based debate that takes note of and develops the research as it is conducted in the world's leading *peer-reviewed journals* and book publishers. In addition, as shown in this publication, proponents of *political Islam*, or those who see it as a possible partner for the West in a world of turmoil, also name it as such. In our study, such supporters have their say in detail, as do those scholars whose statistical evidence suggests that there is no connection between *"political Islam"* and support for anti-Western, Islamist terror. But this whole question is then a question of good empiricism and not an a priori political evaluation of which terms should be used and which should not.

Melani Cammett, Political Science Professor at Harvard,[3] for example, explicitly addressed political *Islam* and, more specifically, political values in the Arab world using data from the Arab *Barometer* (Cammett et al., 2020).[4] *In* our presented voices on *political Islam*, the Arab television station *Al Jazeera* also has its say in detail.

Within a few years of the historic Arab uprisings of 2011, Cammett et al. (2020), found popular mobilisation dissipating amid instability in many Arab countries. In doing so, Cammett and her team tracked the relationship between changing macro-political conditions and individual-level political values in the Middle East, showing that a preference for democracy and political trust are not fixed cultural traits of the population, but can change rapidly in the face of perceived uncertainty. Cammett's empirical analyses use longitudinal data from the for 13 countries as well as data from the *World Values Survey* 2015, which includes both Arab and non-Arab countries, to compare regional developments with global patterns. This basic model is also applied in our study. Cammett's findings contradict cultural studies accounts of

---

[3] Clarence Dillon Professor of International Affairs in the Department of Government Harvard Chan School of Public Health, Acting Director, Weatherhead Center for International Affairs; https://cmes.fas.harvard.edu/people/melani-cammett.

[4] https://scholar.google.com/citations?hl=en&user=CqNmnVwAAAAJ&view_op=list_works.

fixed political attitudes among Muslims in a narrow perspective on the relationship between Islam and democracy. Our analysis starts with such quantitatively and statistically measurable conclusions from international value research and will sometimes reveal very surprising empirical results for the international debate, which sometimes diametrically contradict ideologically shaped expectations from all possible sides.

So what can the readers of our study expect? In this publication, we attempt to empirically shed light on the following research questions, based on established international surveys and data collections, and thus provide an objective contribution to the ongoing debate:

(1) We show with the data of the *"Arab Barometer Survey"* explicitly referring to it how strongly *political Islam* is rooted in the Arab world among the Arab population as a whole and then compare it with the *political Islam of* those who have said in the *Arab Barometer* surveys that they want to emigrate to Western Europe (according to the data presented here, this is more than 1/5 of the entire Arab population). Would continued migration from the Arab world lead to an "import" of *"political Islam"*, or would it be precisely those who do not share the values of *"political Islam"* who want to emigrate, as a high-profile study by Falco and Rotondi, 2016b, in the renowned journal *"World Development"* explicitly claimed? We also examine the multivariate correlates of *"political Islam"* in a factor analytic model that, among other things, explores the question of what correlations exist between an endorsement of *political Islam*, attitudes towards restrictive gender norms (UNDP, 2019) and explicit support for Islamist terror against the United States of America.

(2) Then, using data from the *World Values Survey*, 2017–2020 and the items *"political violence is justified"* and *"in a democracy, religious authorities should interpret the laws"*, *we* show how high the proportion of the total population and of Muslims internationally is that corresponds to these categories, and we ask ourselves in a multivariate comparative analysis with 79 states about the drivers of a readiness to use political violence understood in this way across denominational boundaries, which coincides with a religious sovereignty of interpretation in the legislative process. For the debate on *political Islam, this raises* the not insignificant question that internationally, and also among other denominations, and not only in the *"Dar al Islam"*, i.e. in the House of Islam, a fundamental pillar of the secular constitutional state, namely the renunciation of political violence and the monopoly of state, and not religious, authorities in the interpretation of laws, is rejected by a certain percentage of the population worldwide.

Open Access This chapter is licensed under the terms of the Creative Commons Attribution 4.0 International License (http://creativecommons.org/licenses/by/4.0/), which permits use, sharing, adaptation, distribution and reproduction in any medium or format, as long as you give appropriate credit to the original author(s) and the source, provide a link to the Creative Commons license and indicate if changes were made.

The images or other third party material in this chapter are included in the chapter's Creative Commons license, unless indicated otherwise in a credit line to the material. If material is not included in the chapter's Creative Commons license and your intended use is not permitted by statutory regulation or exceeds the permitted use, you will need to obtain permission directly from the copyright holder.

Chapter 2
"*Political Islam*"—A Contested Term

Abstract This chapter shows that there is a very broad consensus in research in the leading peer-reviewed journals of the social sciences and in the publications of the world's leading book publishers to work with the concept of "political Islam", whereby this analytical-conceptual consensus also includes those who, such as former US President Barack Obama, in his famous Presidential Study Directive No 11, even see an opportunity for cooperation with political Islam, which rejects terrorism, or the French sociologist Francois Burgat, who aggressively argues for an alliance of political Islam with the political left of the West. Important research figures in international Middle East studies, such as Francois Burgat, but also Jocelyne Cesari, John Esposito, Gilles Kepel, Oliver Roy, all of them, and for all the differences they may have in their approach to the phenomenon, have all written important texts on political Islam. We strongly oppose the fact that the Federal Agency for Civic Education (Bundeszentrale für politische Bildung), which is subordinate to the German Ministry of the Interior, writes that whoever uses this term is engaging in "alarmist thinking, placing Muslims under a "general suspicion", fishing in the right-wing pond of voters, and using a term that has incitement potential". This view, expressed by the Federal Agency for Civic Education in Bonn in the language that is so common in Europe today and that covers large sections of the academic community and the opinion columns of the major daily newspapers, seems to be becoming more and more popular.

Keywords Political Islam · Religiously motivated political extremism · Arab Barometer · World Values Survey · Opinion surveys in the Arab world · US foreign policy · Middle East conflict · Federal Republic of Germany · Bundeszentrale für politische Bildung

Now, there are opposing voices against research such as we are aiming at here. I do not need to list all the press commentaries on this topic in a collection of quotations, even in such respected media as the "*NZZ*", the "*Süddeutsche*" and the "*Welt*". Today, as a European "normal citizen", as it should be in the model case, I first turn to the exemplary, *best-practice* European authority responsible for "*political education*"

© The Author(s) 2023
A. Tausch, *Political Islam and Religiously Motivated Political Extremism*,
SpringerBriefs in Political Science,
https://doi.org/10.1007/978-3-031-24854-2_2

in Europe, namely the *Federal Agency for Civic Education in* Bonn, FRG, which is subordinate to the German Federal Ministry of the Interior in Berlin, I receive a downright devastating answer. In the relevant publication of the *"Bundeszentrale"*, Christian Meier, Islamic scholar and historian and since 2016 also editor of the Frankfurt *F.A.Z.*, warns[1] with final and ultimate clarity against using the term *"political Islam"* at all, and whoever uses this term nevertheless, is committing to alarmist thinking, placing Muslims under a "general suspicion", fishing in the right-wing voters' pond and using a term that has incitement potential. The original quote of the corresponding article of the Federal Agency for Civic Education reads as follows, and dozens of press articles have repeated these arguments:

"In any case, it is certain that the term "political Islam" has become a fighting term. Its vagueness and openness make it suitable as a collective term for the political activities of Muslims. At the same time, however, this makes it a projection surface for enemy images and anti-Muslim fears—in other words, potentially an instrument of populism. It remains questionable whether all those who use the term are aware of this. [...] Political Islam has become a term of art for Islam haters. [...] An evaluation of the four national daily newspapers F.A.Z., "Süddeutsche Zeitung", "Tageszeitung" and "Welt" shows that the term "political Islam" has been used more and more frequently over the past decade. And not only in absolute numbers, but also in comparison to the frequency with which the term "Islamism" is used (which, however, is still much more common).

"Political Islam" is now usually used in a much more focused way: as a phenomenon that primarily affects Germany and Europe. And it is often linked to the activities of institutionally organised Muslims in these countries—the so-called Islamic associations. The thrust is—unsurprisingly given the polarisation of any kind of debate about Islam—strongly critical to alarmist. This line can be traced back at least to November 2016, when the CSU adopted the guiding motion "Political Islam" at its party conference, which began with the sentence: "Political Islam is the greatest challenge of our time.

Criticism of the use of the term has not been absent. It is mainly aimed at the lack of or inadequate definition of what "political Islam" is supposed to be. Instead, Muslims are placed under "general suspicion", it is said. Politicians would take advantage of the unclear term and its proximity to "Islam" and in this way "fish in the right-wing voters' pond". [...] In Germany, meanwhile, the president of the Central Committee of German Catholics, Thomas Sternberg, stated that he was critical of the term: It has incitement potential because it confuses politics with violence."

The internationally renowned younger Austrian political scientist Farid Hafez (Bayraklı, & Hafez, 2018; Hafez, 2014), together with the IGGÖ (Islamic Religious Community of Austria), is one of the harshest critics of the use of the term *"political Islam"*.[2] Under the title *"Are France and Austria waging a war against 'political*

---

[1] https://www.bpb.de/politik/extremismus/radikalisierungspraevention/326260/was-ist-eigentlich-unter-politischem-islam-zu-verstehen.

[2] https://www.diepresse.com/5902934/die-heftige-debatte-um-den-politischen-islam. In a long and very readable interview, which shows Farid Hafez to be an undoubtedly outstanding expert

Islam' - or a war against Muslims?", Farid Hafez concisely summarised his arguments in the left-liberal Israeli daily *Haaretz* on 4 April 2021.[3] Farid Hafez says there is a loud controversy about a law drafted by the French government that aims to combat Islamic "separatism" and violent radicalism, but which critics, according to Hafez, accuse of being a clear example of the assumption of collective guilt of all French Muslims for murder, of the denial of individual rights and of state-supported Islamophobia. But at least there is a vigorous national debate about it in France and beyond. According to Hafez, a similar campaign is being waged against the Muslim community in Austria, but with far less media amplification or public solidarity. After 9/11, Hafez said, Austria's political elite used its Muslim population as an example of *"good, domesticated Muslims"*.[4]

2.1 The Scientific GPS for the Analysis of Politics in the Middle East

Our coordinate system of Middle Eastern political forces is based, and we are happy to put this bluntly, exclusively on the annual report of the Institute for National Security Studies in Tel Aviv, Israel (INSS, 2020), known as the *"Strategic Survey for Israel 2019"*. With the INSS, one of the Jewish state's leading security think tanks, we see the following political forces at work in the Gulf region and the greater Middle East, and we supplement this general coordinate system of the region with our own empirical data and background information, as we have worked up in particular in Tausch (2021).

- **The radical Shiite axis**: This cluster is led by Iran and includes Bashar al-Assad's Syria, Hezbollah, the Houthis in Yemen, the Shiite militias operating in various arenas in the Middle East and the Palestinian Islamic Jihad (despite its Sunni identity). A direct estimate of the strength of support for this camp among the Arab public can be derived from the latest version of the Arab Opinion Index (2020) produced by the Arab Center for Research and Policy Studies (ACPRS) in Doha, Qatar. 25% of all residents surveyed in thirteen Arab countries and territories (= West Bank + Gaza) are behind this current. Supporters view Iranian foreign

---

on developments in the region, Farid Hafez speaks of *"political Islam"* being "dead"; cf. https://kopfumkrone.at/kultur/farid-hafez-der-politische-islam-ist-tot. On the considerable, measurable impact of Farid Hafez in international political science, cf. the *open access* bibliometric sources http://classify.oclc.org/classify2/ClassifyDemo?search-author-txt=%22Hafez%2C+Farid%22; https://opensyllabus.org/result/author?id=Farid+Hafez (would, however, have to be corrected for namesake), as well as https://scholar.google.de/citations?user=PYKDme4AAAAJ&hl=de&oi=ao. The left-liberal Israeli daily Haaretz has also reprinted numerous other of Farid Hafez's comments, cf. https://www.haaretz.com/misc/writers/WRITER-1.5603182.

[3] https://www.haaretz.com/world-news/.premium-are-france-and-austria-fighting-A-war-on-terror-or-A-war-on-muslims-1.9655265.

[4] The author refers here to the Israeli website https://www.terrorism-info.org.il/en/for the study of radical Islamist and terrorist movements; operated by the Meir Amit Intelligence and Terrorism Information Center at the Israeli Intelligence Heritage and Commemoration Center.

policy (very) positively. The resistance of the Arab public to this camp is now really considerable. 58% see Iranian foreign policy negatively, and 12% believe that Iran is the greatest security threat to the Arab world today.

- **The pragmatic Sunni states**: This bloc includes Egypt, Jordan, Morocco, Saudi Arabia, the United Arab Emirates and other Arab Gulf states. The author of this study very clearly advocates improved cooperation between Europe and these countries, including in more sensitive areas of foreign and security policy. These actors promote a pro-Western, anti-Iranian, anti-Islamist and nationalist vision. Using data from the Arab Barometer, we find that population-weighted 41% of all Arabs now view the Muslim Brotherhood, which is the strongest and most coherent force in *political Islam*, negatively or very negatively. When weighted by the total population in Arab countries, only 7% of people in Egypt, Iraq, Jordan, Libya, Morocco, Gaza and the West Bank, Sudan, Tunisia and Yemen now have a high level of confidence in their country's Islamist movement (source of summary; both by Arab Barometer), while 14% have some confidence, 19% little confidence but 60% no confidence.
- **The Sunni Islamists**: This group includes adherents of Muslim Brotherhood-style *"political Islam"*[5]: Turkey and certainly Hamas and the remnants of the Muslim Brotherhood and its derivative movements throughout the region, such as Ennahda, the political party in Tunisia, belong to this camp (see also Solomon & Tausch, 2020, 2021). Data from the Arab Barometer suggest that 49% of all Arabs still view the leader of contemporary Sunni Islamism, Turkish President Recep Tayyip Erdoğan, favourably. However, general support for the Muslim Brotherhood and other Islamist political forces has declined sharply in recent years: Support for Hezbollah, the Muslim Brotherhood and Hamas has fallen in public opinion in the years since the Arab uprisings, research by *BBC News Arabic* has found. The English-language newspaper *The National (UAE)*, writes about this with unparalleled clarity: *"More than 25,000 Arabs in 11 states and territories - Morocco, Algeria, Tunisia, Libya, Egypt, Palestine, Yemen, Jordan, Iraq, Sudan and Lebanon - were asked their views on everything from religion to mental health and homosexuality to the role of women in society. A sharp decline in trust for groups espousing political and radical Islam was among the key findings. There has been a marked overall decline in trust in political Islam. [...] This pattern continues a general trend of loss of trust for Islamists in Mena states that has taken place across the region since the Arab uprisings. [...] Despite the initial success of Islamist movements in Egypt and Tunisia, there is growing evidence that Islamism has been in decline over the past eight years."* The National (UAE), 24 June 2019, available at https://www.thenationalnews.com/trust-in-radical-islamist-movements-plummets-major-survey-finds-1.878578
- **The jihadists**: This camp includes the Islamic State (ISIS) and Al-Qaeda, as well as their associated terrorist organisations. According to the latest Arab Opinion

---

[5] The studies in this publication, ranging from proponents to opponents of *"political Islam"*, agree on the extension of the term: the Muslim Brotherhood, Ennahda in Tunisia and the AKP in Turkey in the current phase can be described as *"political Islam"*.

Index by the ACPSR in Qatar, 3% of all Arabs now openly and strongly support ISIL (Daesh), and 2% support it to some extent. Support for ISIL (Daesh) has been declining since 2014, when 4% of all residents of the Arab world viewed ISIL (Daesh) very positively and another 7% viewed ISIL (Daesh) somewhat positively.

2.2 Political Islam

John L. Esposito, Professor of Religion and International Affairs and Islamic Studies at Georgetown University in Washington, DC, and Founding Director of the Prince Alwaleed Centre for Muslim-Christian Understanding at Georgetown Jesuit University, wrote in 2012 with crystal clarity that the phenomenon known as *political Islam* has its roots in a contemporary religious resurgence in private and public life. Esposito, in 2012, also gave a list of political movements that he called political Islamic movements, which is clear and still relevant today, and is used congruently by a wide range of other authors cited in this study. Far from using a purely "fighting term", Esposito referred to the following movements as representing *"political Islam"*:

- The Muslim Brotherhood in Egypt, Sudan and Jordan
- Jamaat-i-Islami in South Asia
- The Refah Party in Turkey
- The Islamic Salvation Front in Algeria
- al Nahda in Tunisia
- Hizballah in Lebanon
- Hamas and Islamic Jihad in the Palestinian territories and
- Gamaa Islamiyya and Jihad in Egypt.

Esposito (2012) added at the time that the causes of the resurgence were religious-cultural, political and socio-economic. Issues of faith, politics and social justice—authoritarianism, oppression, unemployment, housing, social services, distribution of wealth and corruption—would intertwine as catalysts.

In the Arab public political debate, the term *"political Islam"* is of course used just as frequently. For reasons of space, our presentation can probably only be like an express train. Especially the media and academic institutions in the Gulf states, including Qatar, frequently use the term *"political Islam"*. Under the title "Where is *political Islam* headed?", for example, Khalil al-Anani, Associate Professor of political science at the Doha Institute for Graduate Studies in Qatar (https://www.aljazeera.com/opinions/2013/12/24/whither-political-islam) writes on *al Jazeera* that the demise of the Egyptian Muslim Brotherhood (MB) has brought *political Islam* to a crossroad. It has shown not only that ideology in itself is no guarantee of political success, but also that Islamists need to rethink their strategy and tactics to cope with the new post-Arab Spring environment. However, the debate about the end of *political Islam* in the Middle East is not only premature, but also irrelevant and certainly misleading. Instead, it would be more effective to discuss the ideological and political changes that might occur within Islamist movements during the crisis period.

Crystal clear, al-Anani also sees that the majority of Islamist movements in the Arab world maintain a conservative and outdated vision that could not live up to the aspirations and dreams that fuelled the Arab Spring years ago.

Al Jazeera spoke on 21 May 2016, https://www.aljazeera.com/news/2016/5/21/tunisias-ennahda-distances-itself-from-political-islam also about Tunisia, for example, and says Tunisia's conservative Ennahda party says it has *"severed ties" with* any *"political Islam"*. Khaled Abou El Fadl, Distinguished Professor of Law at the University of California Los Angeles (UCLA) School of Law and Chair of the Interdepartmental Programme in Islamic Studies at UCLA, in his commentary on *al Jazeera, which is* still readable today (https://www.aljazeera.com/opinions/2013/7/8/egypt-is-political-islam-dead), says, among other things, that after the military coup in Egypt, many commentators concluded that *"political Islam has been dealt a death blow"* from which such movements will never recover.

Under the title *"Hard times for the "champion" of political Islam. Erdogan's failures should not bring back crude clichés about the incompatibility of political Islam with democracy"*, respected Turkish Analyst Cengiz Aktar, Senior Scholar at the Istanbul Policy Center, also *on al Jazeera* (https://www.aljazeera.com/opinions/2014/1/30/hard-times-for-champion-of-political-islam), says that Turkey and its ruling Justice and Development Party (AKP) have been going through hard times for some time. As the "champion" of *political Islam* among Muslim countries, Turkey is a "model" for some.

In no uncertain terms, Aktar is almost prophetic in naming the crises on the horizon of *"political Islam"* in Turkey, which have indeed deepened since the publication of his commentary: a triple discrepancy between, as Aktar puts it, foreign activism, democratic credentials at home and shortcomings in economic recovery; a lack of experience in balancing great values with real politics; a mere confessionalism that jeopardises relations with neighbouring countries; an overconfidence, which quickly shifts the focus from strategic ties (membership in the European Union and NATO) to *"global delusions"* such as the dream of becoming a member of the Shanghai Cooperation Council and buying NATO-incompatible Chinese missile systems, unlimited power, the steady erosion of remaining checks and balances at all levels of government. In the aforementioned article, Cengiz Aktar also identifies the basic problems of *"political Islam"* in Turkey today: firstly, the AKP has remained in power for far too long, especially Erdogan, who has fallen prey to the corruption of power that Lord Acton has brought to bear, secondly the overconfidence that came from early successes in the economy, democratic reforms and diplomatic activism and thirdly a growing incompetence resulting from Erdogan's one-man show and lack of teamwork. Aktar also speaks of the dismal state of *political Islam* after the Arab Awakening and that the intellectuals who give credit to the ruling AKP are actually useful idiots for the ruling party.

Confronted with this view in the leading medium of the Arab world, which broadcasts from Qatar, we therefore want to try to present objective and comprehensible data on the topic of *"political Islam"*. In doing so, we refer to proven and trustworthy, freely available international opinion polls and want to use them to gain new perspectives on the topic of *"political Islam"* in the Arab world and in Western Europe. In particular, we use the "Arab Barometer Survey", which was co-designed by Qatar University, among others.

2.3 "Political Islam" and Its Open Supporters

Perhaps one of the great surprises for the current debate on *"political Islam"* in Europe is that it can be demonstrated that there were and are indeed voices in the *"security establishment"* and in the *think tanks* and research centres of Western countries concerned with the problem who, in the face of the terrorist challenge posed by jihadism, have advocated and continued to advocate working with forces of *"political Islam"* if they embrace democracy and reject terrorist jihadism. In Arena (2017) and Tausch (2021), it was shown that none other than, for example, Commander-in-Chief of the US Armed Forces 2009 to 2017 and 44th President of the United States of America, Barack Obama *himself*, advocated such a perspective. It is irrelevant whether it could be historically proven that his predecessors in office did not also advocate such a position. A report in the newspaper *"Gulf News"*, which is published in the United Arab Emirates, was a leading piece of journalism in this context and was widely commented on in other global media.[6] It was also dealt with accordingly in a hearing in the American Congress.[7] These reports, which were never questioned by the Democratic Party, said that in the last decade two successive US administrations had close ties to the Muslim Brotherhood in the United Arab Emirates, in Egypt, Tunisia, Syria and Libya. As it was summarised in Tausch, 2021, the Obama administration conducted a new assessment of the Muslim Brotherhood in 2010 and 2011, even before the events known as the "Arab Spring" erupted in Tunisia and Egypt. The president personally issued *Presidential Study Directive 11 (PSD-11) in* 2010, in which he ordered a new assessment of the Muslim Brotherhood and other (literally) *"political Islamist" movements ("political Islamist movements")*, including the ruling AKP in Turkey (Tausch, 2021) and ultimately concluded that the USA should abandon its long-standing policy of supporting "stability" in the Middle East and

---

[6] See, among others: https://www.govinfo.gov/content/pkg/CHRG-114hhrg25270/html/CHRG-114hhrg25270.htm; https://www.washingtontimes.com/news/2015/jun/3/inside-the-ring-muslim-brotherhood-has-obamas-secr/; https://www.scielo.br/j/rbpi/a/k6bDGPqN8NWYsRbxVTmv47n/?lang=en; https://thearabweekly.com/muslim-brotherhood-hopeful-new-obama-era; https://www.investigativeproject.org/documents/testimony/407.pdf; and https://gulfnews.com/world/mena/us-document-reveals-cooperation-between-washington-and-brotherhood-1.1349207.

[7] House Hearing, 114 Congress, From the U.S. Government Publishing Office: IDENTIFYING THE ENEMY: RADICAL ISLAMIST TERROR. HEARING before the SUBCOMMITTEE ON OVERSIGHT AND MANAGEMENT EFFICIENCY of the COMMITTEE ON HOMELAND SECURITY HOUSE OF REPRESENTATIVES ONE HUNDRED FOURTEENTH CONGRESS SECOND SESSION 22 SEPTEMBER 2016, https://www.govinfo.gov/content/pkg/CHRG-114hhrg25270/html/CHRG-114hhrg25270.htm.

North Africa (i.e. supporting "stable regimes" even if they were authoritarian) to a policy of supporting "moderate" Islamist political movements.

To date, Presidential Study Directive PSD-11 has remained secret, because it reveals an embarrassingly naive and uninformed view of developments in the Middle East and North Africa (MENA) region.[8]

There are also other weighty voices in the West that advocate "*political Islam*". In contrast to the uptight discussion, especially in German-speaking countries, however, these voices make no secret of calling the phenomenon by its name—*political Islam*. The shades of academic advocacy of a "*political Islam*" range from the hope for a "*political Islam*" as a partner of the West and in the West's own interest, entirely in the sense of US President Barack Obama's Study Directive PSD-11, to the vision of the overthrow of the capitalist world order, perceived as unjust, by the global political left in explicit alliance with *political Islam*.

The first, politically more moderate position is advocated by the distinguished Canadian political science professor Nader Hashemi, who researches and teaches in Denver, Colorado, in his study "*Political Islam: A 40 Year Retrospective*" (Hashemi, 2021). Nader Hashemi attempts to present a *summa summarum* quite informed analysis of "*political Islam*" and believes that the Western world—in line with President Obama's analysis—should nevertheless see "political *Islam*" as a democratic movement, despite all the failures and undesirable developments that could have been observed in particular in Egypt under President Morsi and in Turkey under President Erdogan with "*political Islam in power*".

The radical vision of the overthrow of the capitalist, world order by the political left in alliance with *political Islam* has been vehemently advocated by, among others, the respected French social scientist Francois Burgat, most recently in Burgat, 2019 (*Understanding Political Islam*).

2.3.1 Political Islam—Not a Gateway Drug to Islamist Terror (Hashemi Study, 2021)

For Hashemi, *political Islam* emerged as a reaction to the decline of Muslim civilisation in the nineteenth and twentieth centuries. Second, according to Hashemi, *political Islamists* (Hashemi, 2021) gradually developed a political theory for a just society based on a critique of secular paradigms and anchored in an argument about Islamic authenticity. Its appeal, according to the aforementioned study, grew over time in direct proportion to the failure of Muslim ruling elites to advance political and economic development. Third, *political Islam* has been an opposition movement for most of its history. Forty years ago, Hashemi argues, *political Islam* had no direct experience of political power or control over state institutions. On this last point, Hashemi says, 2021, much has changed in recent decades, with significant consequences for the future development, attractiveness and orientation of *political Islam*.

---

[8] http://www.alhewar.com/.

2.3 "Political Islam" and Its Open Supporters

Looking back over the last 40 years, the study says, *political Islam*'s experience of political power stands out as an important development.

In his study (2021), Hashemi clarifies where social scientists can study the participation in power of currents and movements of *"political Islam"* in the future—without ifs and buts. In

- Afghanistan
- Egypt
- Gaza
- Iraq
- Iran
- Jordan
- Kuwait
- Malaysia
- Morocco
- Sudan
- Tunisia
- Turkey

had all, according to Hashemi, experienced religiously based political movements contesting political power and gaining control of the state to varying degrees. Without mincing words, Hashemi also names the leading ideologues—without asterisk spelling because they were all men—of *"political Islam"*, namely Hasan Al-Banna (1906–1949), Sayyid Qutb (1906–1966), Abul A'la Maududi (1903–1979) as well as Hasan al-Turabi (1932–2016)[9] (see also Euben and Zaman, 2009).

The Hashemi Study, 2021, makes clear: the reputation of *political Islam* among the population, whose ideology goes back to Hasan Al-Banna, Sayyid Qutb, Abul A'la Maududi as well as Hasan al-Turabi, has been tarnished by his experiences with state power. As an opposition movement, he had once held a high moral position. Its critique of secular ideologies, the political status quo and Western policies towards the Middle East would have appealed to many sections of society. According to Hashemi, in 2021, the Islamist vision of a new political order enjoyed the benefit of the doubt among those who sympathised with its narrative. This has changed markedly since

---

[9] Turabi, the head of the Muslim Brotherhood in Sudan, is seen by some explicit proponents of *"political Islam"* such as Francois Burgat (see below) as a positive figure in the history of contemporary political ideas, see also Taylor, M., & Elbushra, M.E. (2006), and the obituary of Hasan al-Turabi in the left-liberal British Guardian, https://www.theguardian.com/world/2016/mar/11/hassan-al-turabi-obituary. Turabi was the head of the Muslim Brotherhood in Sudan and for many years the chief ideologue of the repressive military rule under Omar al Bashir, until he fell out with Bashir in 1999. The junta was responsible for the war against the minorities in the then south of the country with 2 million dead and 4 million displaced persons, the most serious human rights violations, among others in Darfur, as well as the training of child soldiers of the *Lord's Resistance Army in* neighbouring Uganda. Turabi was also the driving force in the Sudanese regime's collaboration with Osama Bin Laden, who stayed in the country from 1990 to 1996. Anyway, one could say ironically, it is a colossal achievement to have made it to a nice obituary in one of the leading newspapers of the West as the chief ideologue of a regime responsible for 2 million deaths and 4 million displaced persons!

1980, he said, especially with the interplay and takeover of state power by *political Islamist* movements. According to Hashemi, the waning appeal of *political Islam is most evident in* Iran. Decades of military rule in Sudan, supported by the forces of *political Islam*, Hashemi said, led to similar results. Hashemi, 2021, also argues that *political Islam*'s various experiments in attaining state power have, all in all, cast a negative light on this sociopolitical movement. This claim, the study argues, is particularly true for those cases in which Islamists came to power through revolution (Iran), a military coup (Sudan) or military conquest (Afghanistan). According to Hashemi, in the wake of the Arab Spring, several Arab countries (Egypt, Jordan, Saudi Arabia, Bahrain and the United Arab Emirates) officially banned the Muslim Brotherhood or declared it a terrorist organisation in 2021. But is the Muslim Brotherhood a "gateway drug" to radicalisation or does it act as a *firewall* by limiting violent activities? The latter claim is made by Hashemi, 2021. He argues that proponents of the Muslim Brotherhood's "gateway drug" to terror rarely cite empirical studies to support their claim. The Muslim Brotherhood, Hashemi 2021 argues, is thus criticised not because it is a proponent of violence, but because it is fundamentally opposed to the regional status quo and the political regimes that seek to maintain it. Many of the most prominent proponents of violent revolution in the Arab-Islamic world, from Sayyid Qutb to Abu Musab al-Zarkawi to Ayman al-Zawahiri, were products of prison systems in the Arab-Islamic world where they spent years in prison and were subjected to unspeakable cruelty. It is therefore not surprising that people who have been subjected to prolonged torture and extreme interrogation conclude that violence is a legitimate political tool.

2.3.2 For an Explicit Alliance of the Global Left and Political Islam: Francois Burgat (2019)

The French social scientist and Arabist Francois Burgat, who is respected far beyond the borders of France, has turned the entire debate in the German-speaking countries upside down in his publications and says explicitly, militantly and with brilliant rhetoric that "*political Islam*" should be the ally of the political left of the West in the struggle against the capitalist world order. Jihadism only represents a "counter-violence" against the unjust world order. Islamism and jihadism are above all mass protests by self-confident political, often revolutionary actors. This would all have to do with post-colonial suffering, the identification of youth with the "Palestinian cause", the rejection of Western interventions in the Middle East and the rejection of France, which Burgat describes as racist and Islamophobic.

Francois Burgat, who has lived in the region for more than four decades and who cannot be accused of not knowing the Middle East, has in many of his publications, which have been very widely received internationally, among others in Burgat, 2003 (*Face to face with political Islam*), Burgat, 2016 (*Comprendre l'islam politique: une trajectoire de recherche sur l'altérité islamiste, 1973–2016*) and most recently in Burgat, 2019 (*Understanding Political Islam*), he not only explicitly uses the term *"political Islam" with a* positive connotation, but he vehemently pleads for a global alliance of the political left with *"political Islam" in order* to overcome the capitalist world order, which he perceives as corrupted. For him, *"political Islam" is* a tremendously important bearer of hope for overturning this unjust world order and the most important voice of protest today from the Global South.[10] With all the force of his language, Burgat says completely unapologetically that he is **for** *"political Islam" and that the* global and also the European left should enter into an alliance with it.

For Burgat, the spectrum of *political Islam* includes violent terrorist groups such as Al-Qaeda and the Islamic State (IS) as well as Egypt's Muslim Brotherhood and such parties as Tunisia's Ennahda. Burgat, in sharp contrast to the internationally equally high-profile French Islam researcher Gilles Kepel (cf. Kepel, 2002), is in favour of a qualitatively different explanation of Islamism and jihadism. Burgat's starting point is what he calls Western imperialism, the legacy of colonialism and neo-colonialism and the persistent racism and discrimination against Muslims in European societies. Burgat wants to recontextualise Islamism and jihadism. Much of the Western approach to Islamism and jihadism is like *"trees hiding the political forest"* and misleadingly substitutes religious, ideological, psychological or psychosocial causes for fundamentally political ones. Francois Burgat's core demand: the West must end its support for Israel. The radical nature of Burgat's thinking is also evident in an article he published in *"Middle East Eye"*,[11] a platform close to the Muslim Brotherhood, according to the UAE-based daily newspaper *"The National"*. Burgat identifies with the basic direction of *political Islam* in Iran and Sudan under Bashir's military rule. He also finds words of praise for opposition groups like the FIS in Algeria and Islamist currents in Lebanon and Tunisia.

Supporters and opponents of Burgat's analysis must be aware that Burgat also identifies with Hamas, which, as we know, is classified as a terrorist organisation by the European Union.[12]

In the following, we will concentrate on what the international empirical social science sources have to say about the whole complex of problems.

---

[10] https://www.middleeasteye.net/opinion/france-islam-leftist-demonised-antidote; and the article *"Why the West seeks to vilify political Islam"* by Alain Gabon Professor of French Studies and Department Head for Foreign Languages & Literatures at Virginia Wesleyan University in Virginia Beach, USA, downloadable at https://www.middleeasteye.net/opinion/why-west-seeks-vilify-politi cal-islam, which excellently summarises Burgat's theses. The author of this study is deeply indebted to this summary of Francois Burgat's extensive work.

[11] https://www.thenationalnews.com/uae/new-london-connection-to-islamists-1.648408.

[12] https://www.dw.com/en/eu-court-rejects-hamas-appeal-to-delist-terrorist-status/a-47790588.

Open Access This chapter is licensed under the terms of the Creative Commons Attribution 4.0 International License (http://creativecommons.org/licenses/by/4.0/), which permits use, sharing, adaptation, distribution and reproduction in any medium or format, as long as you give appropriate credit to the original author(s) and the source, provide a link to the Creative Commons license and indicate if changes were made.

The images or other third party material in this chapter are included in the chapter's Creative Commons license, unless indicated otherwise in a credit line to the material. If material is not included in the chapter's Creative Commons license and your intended use is not permitted by statutory regulation or exceeds the permitted use, you will need to obtain permission directly from the copyright holder.

Chapter 3
The Scientific Background to Our Own Empirical Study

Abstract In this chapter, we amply debate the contributions on "political Islam" in the leading peer-reviewed journals of social science. We discuss contributions by Francois Burgat, but also Jocelyne Cesari, John Esposito, Gilles Kepel and Oliver Roy clearly outline which important value patterns the adherents of political Islam represent (five items from the Arab Barometer) and which political movements and governments of countries are to be assigned to the extension of the phenomenon. Of special importance is the study by Harvard Professor Melanie Cammett (Cammett et al., 2020), which deals explicitly with political Islam and political values in the Arab world using data from the Arab Barometer. The empirical analyses of Cammett et al. (2020), use longitudinal data from the Arab Barometer as well as data from the World Values Survey 2015. We also debate the contributions by such authors as Fox et al. (2016), Achilov (2016); as well as empirical contributions by Driessen (2018), Kucinskas and Van Der Does (2017); a highly interesting Iranian paper, authored by Rahbarqazi and Mahmoudoghli (2020); and the Tessler (2010), study. All these studies were very valuable in the formation of our own empirical research.

Keywords Political Islam · Religiously motivated political extremism · Arab Barometer · World Values Survey · Opinion surveys in the Arab world · Empirical political science research · Middle East research · Scopus

Piece by piece, we now want to work out the scientific background to our own empirical study. First of all, we need to clarify the role of *"political Islam"* in the global flagship of Arab opinion research.

The following *studies on "political Islam" have been* cited more than 50 times in the international literature recorded in the *Scopus* database:

Baswedan (2004), Blaydes and Linzer (2010, 2012), de Soysa and Nordås (2007), Fleischmann and et al. (2011), Gülalp (2001), Gumuscu (2010), Mecham (2004), Öniş (2001), Özbudun (2006).

3.1 Political Islam: The Information Potential of Fox's et al. (2016) and Achilov's (2016) Studies on Political Islam Based on the Arab Barometer

Fox et al. (2016), in an excellent, and much-cited paper, analysed Arab Barometer data to find out the relationship between gender attitudes and overall political attitudes. Using available data from successive rounds of the Arab *Barometer survey*, Fox et al. (2016), examined changes in attitudes in nine countries with two rounds of Arab *Barometer* data during and after the Arab Spring (Egypt, Yemen, Tunisia, Algeria, Lebanon, Sudan, Jordan, Iraq, West Bank and Gaza). Support for "Muslim feminism" (an interpretation of gender equality grounded in Islam) over the period and especially in Arab Spring countries has increased, while support for "secular feminism" has decreased.

In one of the most promising international studies using Arab Barometer data, Dilshod Achilov (Achilov, 2016) used the following variables to distinguish between politically moderate and politically radical Islam. We use here—for interested readers who want to recalculate Akhilov's analysis—the direct references to the *Arab Barometer* Project questionnaire:

(1) **Support for political pluralism**

(Q246.1)—Parliamentary system in which all political parties (left, right, Islamic) can compete with each other

(Q225.1)—Competition and disagreement between political groups are not bad

(Q255.2)—National leaders should be open to different political ideas.

(2) **Support for individual civil liberties and political rights**

(Q245.1)—Support for a democratic political system (public freedom, equal political rights, balance of power, accountability and transparency)

(Q402.1)—Government and parliament should legislate according to the wishes of the people.

(3) **Accommodative (inclusive) support for both Shariah and secular law**

(Q402.3)—Government and parliament should legislate according to the wishes of the people in some areas and implement Sharia law in others.

(4) **(In-) Tolerance towards political pluralism**

(Q246.2)—A parliamentary system in which only Islamic political parties and factions participate in elections.

Political radical Islam is defined by

(1) **Neglect of democratic elections and competition**

(Q246.4)—A system governed by Islamic law in which there are no political parties or elections

(2) **Exclusive support for the rule of Sharia law and the political influence of the clergy**.

(Q402.2)—The government should only implement Sharia laws

(Q401.1)—Religious dignitaries should have an influence on how people vote in elections

(Q401.3)—Religious dignitaries should have influence over government decisions.

Achilov (2016) conducted a multivariate principal component analysis (i.e. a variant of "factor analysis", cf. below) to empirically examine *political Islam*. In order to control for the "Islamist" aspect of the conceptualisation (hence distinguishing it from more general support for pluralist democracy), only respondents who (1) practise Islam (pray and read the Qur'an) and who (2) believe "religious practice is not a private matter and should not be separated from sociopolitical life" were included in the factor analysis. Achilov (2016), conceptualised two different forms of support for political Islamic ideology: politically moderate and politically radical Islam. Based on multivariate regression analysis, Achilov (2016) concluded that religiosity is important, but its main effects on collective political action are small and highly context dependent. The impact of religiosity on political activism varies across states. Nevertheless, personal piety remains an important factor in explaining collective protests in the MENA region. Muslims with higher levels of ideological support for politically moderate Islam are more likely to participate in non-violent, collective political protests. The collective voice of politically moderate Muslims will be crucial in future. Muslims with higher levels of ideological support for politically radical Islam seem less likely to participate in elite-challenging collective protests.

3.2 The Studies by Falco and Rotondi

Falco and Rotondi (2016a), examined the relationship between political Islam, willingness to migrate and Internet use by exploiting the second (2010–2011) and third (2012–2014) waves of the Arab Barometer. Here, we investigated whether the Internet may act as a vehicle of *political Islam* and willingness to migrate. The results show that there is a positive relationship between Internet use and willingness to migrate at the individual level, while there is a negative relationship between *political Islam* and willingness to migrate at the individual level. The results also show that Internet use does not have a significant impact on *political Islam*. Falco and Rotondi (2016b), examine radical Islam as a determinant of individuals' willingness to migrate. Falco and Rotondi (2016b), quite rightly say that surprisingly, this topic has not been empirically investigated in the literature despite its relevance to the political debate. To fill this gap, Falco and Rotondi (2016b), develop a model of the decision to migrate, focusing in particular on the role of cultural characteristics. In particular, the study focuses on radical Islam as a potential deterrent to migration. It defines radical Islam as a set of ideologies, also referred to as *political Islam.*

Islam should guide not only personal life but also social and political life. In the model, more radical values mean higher psychological migration costs. These costs arise from the fact that connections to socio-religious friends and neighbours are generally not maintained after migration, discouraging individuals from migrating. The study then empirically tests the predictions of the model using individual-level data from the second (2010–11) and third (2012–14) waves of the Arab Barometer. The results suggest that more radical individuals are less likely to migrate, *ceteris paribus*. This finding is robust to alternative specifications of the model and to the use of *instrumental variables* and *propensity score matching to* shed mathematical and statistical light on the potential endogeneity of radical Islam. The result also remains qualitatively unchanged when aggregate data on actual migrant outflows are used.

3.3 The Studies Whose Design Was Important for Our Own Empirical Investigation

3.3.1 The Cammett et al. (2020) Study

Harvard Professor Cammett makes extensive use of the Arab Barometer toolkit in Cammett et al. (2020). First, Cammett argues that preference for democracy is positively associated with national average levels of economic security, as well as with perceptions of economic security and personal security at the individual level. However, the national level of personal security does not play a significant role in shaping preference for democracy. One of the main hypotheses examined here concerns preference for democracy and trust in government in relation to national support for *political Islam*. To test the impact of attitudes towards *political Islam* in the data set, Cammett et al. (2020), did so by using two questions in the Arab Barometer: "Is your country better off if religious people hold public positions in the state?" and "Religious clerics should have influence over government decisions". However, Cammett et al. (2020), found no relationship between any of the measures of preference for democracy used and attitudes towards *political Islam* at the national level. However, according to Cammett, support for *political Islam* at the individual level and support for democracy were weakly correlated (and within different countries, the results would show weak statistical significance and changing signs).

Cammett et al. (2020), also makes interesting observations about developments in individual countries, although these are beyond the horizon of our own study. In any case, it is essential that such a high-profile international study uses two questions in the Arab Barometer: "Is your country better off when religious people hold public positions in the state?" and "Religious clerics should have influence on government decisions" to measure *political Islam*.

3.3.2 The Cesari Study, 2021

Political Islam and Islamism, according to Cesari, in her article 2021, published in the journal *Religions, are* terms used interchangeably to describe Islamic parties and movements that have gained prominence since the 1960s in opposition to "secular" states. Most scholarship discusses the democratic dimension of these parties, their ability to fit into the mainstream political system, and their propensity for violence for political purposes, both nationally and internationally. The rich literature on the Muslim Brotherhood in different national contexts is paradigmatic of this dominant perception of Islamism, according to Cesari (2021). Interestingly, there are also studies on the interactions between the state and Islam (Cesari refers here to the important studies by Fox (2019), Driessen (2014), Henne (2012)).

According to Cesari (2021), Islamism emerged as a reaction to the decline of "Muslim civilisation" and was supplemented by a political theory of a just society based on Islamic authenticity and criticism of secularism. It was, according to Cesari (2021), an opposition movement to the "secular" state and was therefore able to maintain the moral upper hand. But in the last four decades, Islamism had become part of political power, from Iran to Morocco and Tunisia. This has eroded its political credibility, he says, especially where state power has been won by force (as in Iran, Sudan and Afghanistan), not to mention the odious reputation that the claim of an "Islamic state" has received from ISIS. Overall, according to Cesari (2021), Islamist parties show a poor record of gaining state power, a situation discussed at length by scholars who look for structural obstacles to explain such failure from the persistence of deep state power or the degree of corruption and dysfunctionality of state institutions. Human rights violations and authoritarianism in countries such as Iran, Sudan and Afghanistan have further undermined the reputation of Islamists.

In contrast, Islamists who have come to power through elections have greater legitimacy but, according to Cesari (2021), face similar structural challenges and are seeing an erosion of their popular support, as evidenced by the situations in Turkey, Tunisia and Egypt. The academic consensus, according to Cesari (2021), is that popular support for Islamism has currently peaked and is unlikely to rise further, as opinion polls show a significant decline in support for religious parties and leaders, most of them in Arab countries.

Cesari (2021), identifies the question of whether "*political Islam*" is a "gateway drug" to political violence (cf. also the study by Hashemi, 2021, referred to here) as the crucial question in the context. The gateway drug thesis postulates that the Muslim Brotherhood acts as a gateway to radical fundamentalism, although, as Cesari (2021) says, the organisation has rejected violence as a means of political power. Because this so-called thesis is politically influential, it forces scholars to mobilise their expertise to refute it. This explicit or implicit struggle with an "ideological opponent" is, according to Cesari (2021), a serious limitation for all scholarship on Islamism/political *Islam*, as it often turns into apologetics or hostility towards the topics or subjects under study. The empirical reality, he said, is that Islamism is multifaceted and can be a gateway to a more democratic and pluralistic worldview, just as it can be a gateway to radicalism. The main aim in Cesari's study (Cesari, 2021) is to distinguish *political Islam* from Islamism and to consider the former as more comprehensive and long term than the latter. *Political Islam*, he argues, is better defined as a political culture that is the result of the dual process of nationalisation and reformation of the Islamic tradition. We are therefore better advised, says Cesari, 2021, to consider *political Islam* as governmentality[1] and **Islamism as the religiously based form of political mobilisation that is** one of the many outcomes of that *governmentality*. Incidentally, Cesari (2021), is harsh in her judgement of Turkey under Erdogan: according to Cesari, the AKP promoted the idea of a "Muslim democracy" (as opposed to the Islamic State claimed by most Islamist movements). In doing so, it fuelled the hope that Islam could harbour and even forge a new kind of democracy, independent of the Western model. This hope has been undermined in recent years, Cesari argues, by Recep Tayyip Erdogan's turn towards authoritarianism, not to mention his attempts to combine Islam and nationalism by legitimising the headscarf in public spaces or tightening presidential control over the religious authority Diyanet. According to Cesari (2021), such a development contradicts the historically grown perception of Turkey as a country with a "westernised" political power. Turkey had entered into competition with other Islamic countries such as Saudi Arabia or Iran for the leadership of the *Ummah*. Global *political Islam*, especially in its radical forms, is, according to Cesari (2021), the result of the spread and transformation of the aforementioned hegemonic political cultures.

---

[1] According to the Encyclopaedia Britannica, governmentality is described as follows: "*Governmentality, approach to the study of power that emphasizes the governing of people's conduct through positive means rather than the sovereign power to formulate the law.* **In contrast to a disciplinarian form of power, governmentality is generally associated with the willing participation of the governed.** *The concept of governmentality takes the definition of government as the exercise of organised political power by a nation or state (see also nation-state) and expands it to include the* **active consent and willingness of individuals to participate in their own governance***. It proposes that government by the state is only one form of governing, that the terms state and government are not synonymous, and that actions taken by the state alone cannot bring about its desired ends. Governmentality, an expression originally formulated by the 20th-century French philosopher Michel Foucault, combines the terms* **government and rationality**. *Government in this sense refers to conduct, or an activity meant to shape, guide, or affect the conduct of people. Conduct takes on meaning beyond the form of leading and directing. It also refers to the "conduct of oneself" where a sense of self-governance is a guiding force. Rationality, as a form of thinking that strives to be systematic and clear about how things are or ought to be, suggests that before people or things can be controlled or managed, they must first be defined. Therefore, the state designs systems for defining populations, which make them known and visible. They include mechanisms of management and administration (work processes, procedures, rules) and ways of classifying individuals or groups (by income, race, professional and personnel categories), which allow for their identification, classification, ordering, and control*". https://www.britannica.com/topic/governmentality.

3.3.3 The Driessen (2018) Study

Scholars of *political Islam* (sic), according to Mihael D. Driessen, Professor at the Department of Political Science and International Affairs, John Cabot University, in Rome, have observed how a new generation of Muslim political actors have combined religious ideals and democratic institutions in their evolving political visions, platforms and policies. Driessen's study documented in its findings the pronounced and widespread demand that exists in the Muslim-majority world for a combination of Sharia law and democratic politics. To this end, Driessen (2018), used regression analyses to analyse the relationship between religious regulation measures and religious *favouritism* (on the two terms, below) with *World Values Survey* Wave 4 data (1999–2004) and *Arab Barometer survey data* from Wave 2 (2010–2011) and Wave 3 (2012–2014). Driessen paid attention in order to capture the difference between religious regulation and religious *favouritism*. Religious favouritism happens […] when a state identifies with and subsidises certain religious symbols, values, schools and holy days. However, religious regulation that enforces certain individual religious beliefs, suppresses religious minorities and does not consensually interfere with the institutional or theological structures of religious organisations violates these procedural democratic rights. While social scientists have found a strong and negative relationship between religious regulation and democracy, there is no systematic relationship between religious favouritism and democracy. Once religious regulation is controlled for, there is little statistical evidence of a relationship between religious favouritism and democracy, and many democracies institutionalise moderate to high levels of religious favouritism (Driessen, 2018).

Religious regulation corresponds to the later questions about *"political Islam"* used in the *Arab Barometer*. The Driessen study, 2018, argues that the strong support of most Muslim populations for both democracy and Sharia law has led to a common, clear pattern of support for indirect channels of religious influence in a democratic context. Most Muslim individuals in Muslim-majority countries appear to simultaneously desire a continued public presence of religion in the state, but also want policy-making to be in the hands of elected individuals (whom Muslim citizens hope is personally pious) as opposed to unelected religious authorities (whom they want to keep out of government business).

With this argument, Driessen (2018), adds his study to a growing number of scholars who recognise the emergence of a version of Muslim democracy as a key feature of contemporary Muslim politics.

3.3.4 The Kucinskas and Van Der Does (2017) Study

Using *Arab Barometer data* (2011), Kucinskas and Van Der Does (2017), examine the gender attitudes of Muslim men in four predominantly Muslim countries in the Middle East and North Africa (Algeria, Egypt, Tunisia and Yemen) during the

Arab Spring. They investigated whether living in insecurity—which can threaten men's ability to achieve masculine ideals—is linked to male overcompensation, as evidenced by strong support for patriarchal gender ideology. They also investigated whether Islamic religiosity influences this relationship. The results show that *political Islam*—as defined by the *Arab Barometer*—is strongly linked to patriarchal gender attitudes among Muslim MENA men across the region. The impact of living in insecurity and other facets of Islamic religiosity on men's gender ideology varies by country. The findings on the multiple impacts of insecurity and Islam on men's gender ideology challenge stereotypical portrayals of the region as uniformly Islamic and patriarchal. Ultimately, according to Kucinskas and Van Der Does (2017), findings point to the pervasive influence of *political Islam* on men's gender ideology in MENA in relation to women. During a period of heightened civil unrest in the four countries studied, Kucinskas and Van Der Does (2017), also see different relationships between insecurity, Islam and male gender ideology depending on the country.

To measure *political Islam* according to *Arab Barometer*, the study used four questions on opinion about the country's laws and regulations (on a four-point Likert scale ranging from "strongly disagree" to "strongly agree"):

"The government and parliament should enact the following laws:

(1) Laws
(2) Criminal laws
(3) Personal status laws and
(4) Inheritance laws in accordance with Islamic laws".

Kucinskas and Van Der Does (2017), supplemented these measures with six additional questions (on the same Likert scale) recoded so that larger scores represent a belief in a greater role for religion in politics:

- "Religious leaders should not interfere in voters' decisions in elections"
- "Your country is better off when religious people hold public positions in the state"
- "Religious leaders should have influence on government decisions"
- "Religious practices are private and should be separated from social and political life"
- "Religious associations and institutions should not influence voters' decisions in elections" and
- "Mosques should not be used for election campaign purposes".

Finally, Kucinskas and Van Der Does (2017), used two questions on the belief that the following political systems are appropriate for one's country, with responses on a four-point Likert scale (from absolutely inappropriate to very appropriate):

- "A parliamentary system in which only Islamist parties contest elections" and
- "A system governed by Islamic law, without elections or political parties".

These twelve questions were standardised before a summated scale with an alpha of 0.75 was created.

A summed scale had a more accurate result than a measure from a factor analysis.

3.3 The Studies Whose Design Was Important for Our Own Empirical … 27

The Arab Barometer questionnaire contained more variables on religious practices, including measures of fasting, reading/watching religious materials, attending religious classes, participating in Friday prayers and reading religious books. These variables attenuate each other due to high collinearity.

Kucinskas and Van Der Does (2017), added control variables that have been shown to influence men's gender ideology

- Age (in years)
- University education (1 = has a B.A. or M.A. or higher, 0 = has no university education) and
- Marital status (1 = not married, 0 = married).

Kucinskas and Van Der Does (2017), also take into account whether the respondent lives in a rural (1) or urban (0) area. Finally, to control for country-specific differences in development and economic conditions, Kucinskas and Van Der Does (2017), added to the models the Human Development Index (HDI) values for each country from the United Nations Development Programme Human Development Report (2011).

Kucinskas and Van Der Does (2017), found support for the expectation that religious men would be more supportive of patriarchal gender ideology. Some facets of Islam in certain contexts, such as, according to Kucinskas and Van Der Does (2017), the self-identified religiosity of Egyptian men, the self-identified frequent reading of the Qur'an by Yemeni men and the daily prayer of Algerian men, are associated with stronger patriarchal attitudes. In Egypt, according to Kucinskas and Van Der Does (2017), men who read the Quran weekly have less patriarchal attitudes than others. The only consistent finding by country is the positive impact of *political Islam* on patriarchal gender ideology. In all countries, men's belief that Islam should influence politics and governance was associated with patriarchal attitudes. This finding shows the importance of not only considering standard measures of religious affiliation, belief and behaviour, but also the influence of politically shaped religious beliefs.

The impact of *political Islam* on gender ideology in Egypt is significantly lower than in the other countries. The impact of *political Islam* in Tunisia was, according to Kucinskas and Van Der Does (2017), lower than in Yemen and Algeria. *Political Islam* plays a role in shaping gender ideology in different countries, but not to the same extent. The findings of Kucinskas and Van Der Does (2017), lead to as Kucinskas and Van Der Does (2017), themselves say—losing their own confidence in most of their findings presented. The only robust, consistent finding across countries, according to Kucinskas and Van Der Does (2017), shows the strong relationship between *political Islam* and men's patriarchal gender ideology.

3.3.5 *The Rahbarqazi and Mahmoudoghli (2020) Study*

The following study, which also interprets *Arab Barometer* data in an exemplary manner, is another example of the use of multivariate analysis to study *political Islam*.

The study in itself is an event because of its very good theoretical and statistical-empirical treatment of the subject, which has also found its way into the renowned *"Revista Espanola de Sociología"*, but it deserves to be published in Western Europe, where, as we noted in great detail in our introduction and background chapter, there is a great deal of scepticism about a discourse on *"political Islam"*, it deserves special attention, since the authors are not doing research at any of the Anglo-American universities, but at the University of Isfahan, and at the University of Mohaghegh Ardabili, in Iran. When these authors talk explicitly about *political Islam* in their region, i.e. a system of rule that has been in power in Iran since 1979, it simply has a different quality than the scholarly essay by academics who live in relative safety. With an almost merciless precision, they already say what they are about in the title of their paper published in a renowned Spanish sociology journal: *"Corruption Perceptions, Political Distrust, and the Weakening of Political Islam in Iraq"*.

The study used the Arab Barometer Wave V data from 2018 to 2019. By examining the data of 2461 Iraqi citizens, Rahbarqazi and Mahmoudoghli (2020), results show that corruption perceptions, on the one hand, increase citizens' perceptions of poor government performance and wrong direction of the country and, on the other hand, decrease the tendency for a democratic political system. The results also show, according to our two Iranian authors, that citizens' perceptions of corruption indirectly, through the above three mediating variables, increase political distrust in society and negatively influence *political Islamisation*. Therefore, citizens' perceptions of corruption seem to be one of the important reasons that challenge the public's trust in institutions and the prevailing political ideology.

The ideology that governs Iraq, our quoted Iranian authors say, seems to be *political Islamism*. And this is without inverted commas and without further detours. The authors go on to say that paragraph 1 of Article 2 of the Constitution of the Republic of Iraq (2005) states that "Islam is the official religion of the state". As a result, the study says, immediately in Part A of this constitutional article, "No laws shall be enacted that are contrary to the established provisions of Islam". Probably, according to Rahbarqazi and Mahmoudoghli (2020), this is the reason why Ayatollah Sistani and other religious authorities would easily comment on political matters and can interfere. In many cases, the leadership of political parties and groups in Iraq is also the responsibility of ayatollahs and religious clerics. Given that most political structures in Iraq are held by Islamist political groups or parties close to this ideology, the research hypothesis of Rahbarqazi and Mahmoudoghli (2020), is therefore perceptions of corruption indirectly reduce citizens' support for *political Islam* in Iraq by increasing *political* distrust.

In the study by Rahbarqazi and Mahmoudoghli (2020), which was conducted with the very advanced statistical software package AMOS, multiple regression equations were used. So how does Rahbarqazi and Mahmoudoghli (2020), address the question of how to measure "support for *political Islam*"? According to the Iranian authors Rahbarqazi and Mahmoudoghli (2020), the term refers to a variety of forms of social and political activity that claim that public and political life should be guided by Islamic principles. Respondents' acceptance or rejection of *political Islam* was measured using 4 items on a four-point Likert scale. In this context, respondents were asked to what extent they agreed or disagreed with the following statements:

- **Religious leaders should not interfere in voters' decisions in elections** (1 = I strongly agree, 4 = I strongly disagree, mean = 1.88; Corrected item-total correlation = 0.22)
- **Your country is better off when religious people hold public positions in the state** (1 = I strongly agree, 4 = I strongly disagree, mean = 2.89; Corrected item-total correlation = 0. 34) [reversed]
- **Religious practice is a private matter and should be separated from socio-economic life** (1 = I strongly agree, 4 = I strongly disagree, mean = 1.87; Corrected item-total correlation = 0.28) and
- **Religious leaders today are just as likely to be corrupt as non-religious leaders** (1 = I strongly agree, 4 = I strongly disagree, mean = 1.97; Corrected item-total correlation = 0.26.

While democracy showed a negative relationship with political distrust, the relationship between education level, income status, perception of corruption, poor government performance and a negative impression of the country's future was positive with positive political distrust. Women were also found to be more inclined to *"political Islamism"*, according to the study, than men. But the relationship between education level, perception of corruption, poor government performance, negative perception of the country's future and political distrust was negatively correlated with "political Islamism".

Since *"political Islamism"*, according to the study, has a high influence on the historical, social and political contexts of Middle Eastern societies, religious fundamentalism is presented as a strong alternative to the ruling regimes in the countries of the region. People are increasingly turning to *"political Islamism"*.

3.3.6 The Tessler (2010), Study

As the last of the alphabetically listed studies on *political Islam* based on the *Arab Barometer*, we refer here to the study by Mark Tessler, which is very frequently cited in the literature.

Tessler (2010), stresses that public opinion in the Arab world is characterised by a clear and sharp disagreement on whether Islam should play a role in public affairs or not. Many ordinary men and women favour a separation of religion and politics. This could reflect a desire to protect the political process from religious influence and authority. Alternatively, it could reflect, at least in part, a belief that religion would be corrupted by politics and possibly pressured to make compromises that do not sufficiently respect Islamic codes and traditions. Whatever the reason, the Arab public is divided on this issue. And as this public gains a greater say in the governance of their countries, the place of Islam in political life will surely be one of the most hotly contested issues. Calls for political reform and democratisation are widespread in the Arab world. Significantly, however, the disagreement on the issue of *political Islam* has not had as much impact on democratisation as might be expected. On the one hand, Tessler says in his famous study, an overwhelming majority of citizens who favour a political role for Islam, like the vast majority of those who favour a separation of religion and politics, believe that democracy, whatever its flaws and limitations, is the best form of government and the one they would most like to see established in their own country. In other words, there is, according to Tessler, broad support for democracy across the Arab world, and this is the case among those who do not believe, but also and equally among those who believe that Islam should play a role in political affairs. Tessler shows this empirically with very simple comparisons across the batteries of questions in the *Arab Barometer*, first comparing support for or rejection of democracy in a cross-tabulation with the four classic indicators of "*political Islam*" according to *Arab Barometer* used in the other studies mentioned and also used by us in our own empirical research (see below).

Tessler then shows, also in very simple cross-tabulations, how individuals in the Arab world differ in their opinions on the item "Religious representatives should have an influence on government decisions" (agree (strongly) versus disagree (strongly)).

Gender Equality

- A married woman can work outside the home if she wants to
- Men are generally better political leaders than women
- Men and women should receive equal wages and salaries.

Tolerance
Factors that qualify a person for national leadership:

- Openness to different political ideas
- Islam requires that in a Muslim country, the political rights of non-Muslims are subordinate to those of Muslims
- Which of the following groups would you like to have as neighbours?
- People of a different race or skin colour.

Interpersonal Trust

- Would you say that, in general, most people can be trusted?
- Are you a member of any organisations or formal groups?
- Did you vote in the last national election?
- Did you attend a campaign event or rally during the last national election?
- Have you ever joined with others to draw attention to an issue or sign a petition?

Political Interest

- How interested are you in politics in general?
- How often do you follow news about politics and government?

3.3 The Studies Whose Design Was Important for Our Own Empirical ... 31

Political Knowledge

- Can name the Foreign Minister
- Can name the Speaker of the House.

Tessler says very crucially for his approach, there is the critical division in terms of governance not between those who advocate *political Islam* and those who advocate secular democracy, but between those who advocate secular democracy and those who believe that the political system should be both democratic and Islamic.

On the other hand, there are very few differences in the political culture orientation of Arabs who prefer democracy with Islam and those who prefer secular democracy. According to Tessler, the importance of political culture in developing countries in 2010 is largely due to its relevance for democratisation. With only a few exceptions, notably in Kuwait, there is little difference between the *political culture* orientations of citizens who prefer democracy with Islam and those who prefer a democratic system that does not assign an important role to Islam.

Even if neither support for democracy nor orientation towards political culture differs as a function of attitudes towards *political Islam*, Tessler's famous study argues that it is important to understand the factors that incline ordinary men and women towards one position or another on the question of how their country should be governed. Personal religiosity is clearly the most consistent of these factors. Among the large proportion of Muslim Arabs who support democracy, those with a stronger attachment to their religion, as measured by the frequency of Quran reading and the importance of a child marrying someone who is religious, are disproportionately likely to favour a political system that is Islamic. Beyond this, however, there is little consistency in the factors that lead an individual to support *political Islam*, or in the countries where certain factors play a role in shaping the preferences of the political system. Interpretations of Islamic law, political and economic assessments and personal characteristics and experiences have explanatory power in some cases. The findings, according to Tessler (2010), suggest that one-size-fits-all explanations should be avoided and that it is impossible to answer the question of why some Muslim Arabs prefer democracy with religion, while others favour secular democracy without constructing explanatory models that take into account country-level circumstances and experiences.

Although there is still much to learn, says Tessler (2010), it is possible to conclude with two broad observations that emerge from the findings presented above. Both challenge popular stereotypes and, according to Tessler, may have implications for the way policymakers and others in the West think about *political Islam*. One conclusion is that there is little or no public incompatibility between Islam and democracy. Support for democracy and democratic values is no less present among citizens with a positive attitude towards *political Islam* than among others. The other conclusion, according to Tessler (2010), is that there is no one-dimensional determinism in the Arab world.

Open Access This chapter is licensed under the terms of the Creative Commons Attribution 4.0 International License (http://creativecommons.org/licenses/by/4.0/), which permits use, sharing, adaptation, distribution and reproduction in any medium or format, as long as you give appropriate credit to the original author(s) and the source, provide a link to the Creative Commons license and indicate if changes were made.

The images or other third party material in this chapter are included in the chapter's Creative Commons license, unless indicated otherwise in a credit line to the material. If material is not included in the chapter's Creative Commons license and your intended use is not permitted by statutory regulation or exceeds the permitted use, you will need to obtain permission directly from the copyright holder.

Chapter 4
Methods and Design of Our Own Empirical Study

Abstract The empirical analyses of our study are based on IBM-SPSS-24 promax factor analyses of 24 variables according to the Arab Barometer, explicitly measure political Islam with five variables and also determine the environment (19 variables) of political Islam and its consequences, such as the lack of tolerance towards other religions, identification with states that today clearly represent political Islam, such as the regime in Iran, President Erdogan in Turkey, restrictive gender norms as defined by the UNDP Human Development Report, 2019, the belief that Muslims should enjoy greater rights in a state than non-Muslims, the negative fixation against the USA, UK and Israel in world politics, the call for a Sharia that explicitly introduces corporal punishment and restricts women's rights, and expressing a sympathetic understanding of acts of anti-American terror in the Middle East. In this chapter, we debate the design of our study, the quantitative statistical methodology, the multivariate methods, especially based on promax factor analysis, the error margins, the problem of traceability, and the macro-quantitative cross-national data used in our comparisons. The chapter duly discusses the Arab Barometer and the files of the World Values Survey.

Keywords Political Islam · Religiously motivated political extremism · Arab Barometer · World Values Survey · Opinion surveys in the Arab world · Empirical political science research · Middle East research · Promax factor analysis

In this chapter, we discuss the data sources of our analysis and the statistical methods used. We mention the methods and data in the order in which they appear in this publication.

Our data sources used are the best available opinion polls on Arab countries, hence the *Arab Barometer* and the *World Values Survey*.

4.1 The Survey-Based Methodology in Comparative Social Research and the Potential of the World Values Survey

The *World Values Survey* (www.worldvaluessurvey.org) *is*, according to its website, a global network of social scientists concerned with changing values and their impact on social and political life, led by an international team of scientists. The WVS Association and the Secretariat are based in Stockholm, Sweden and the current President of the WVS Association is, incidentally, the Austrian political scientist Prof. Christian Haerpfer from the University of Vienna, who is very well known in the world's scientific journals.

The WVS survey, which began in 1981, aims to use the most rigorous and highest-quality research designs in each country. The WVS consists—again, according to the official self-conception documented on its website—of nationally representative surveys conducted in nearly 100 countries, home to almost 90% of the world's population, using a common questionnaire. The WVS is the largest non-commercial, cross-national time-series survey of human beliefs and values ever conducted and currently includes interviews with nearly 400,000 respondents. Moreover, the WVS is the only academic study that covers the full range of global differences from very poor to very rich countries in all major cultural zones of the world. Figure 4.1 shows the gigantic geographical spread of this project today. The research has so far taken place in seven different waves, with waves 5 and 6, conducted after 1999, being relevant for Middle East research.

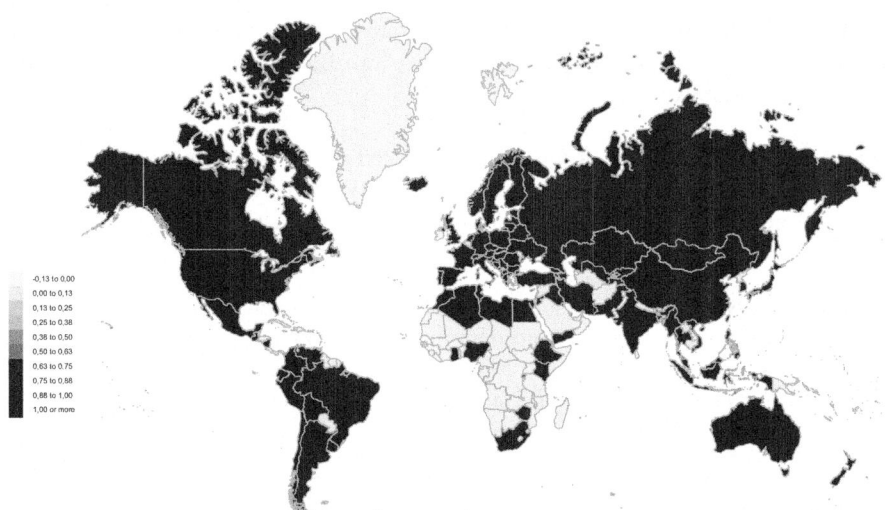

Fig. 4.1 Maximum geographical coverage of the *World Values Survey* in wave 4 (2010–2014) and wave 5 (2017–2020) for multivariate analysis. *Source* Our own SPSS calculations from the data of the *World Values Survey*, https://www.worldvaluessurvey.org/WVSContents.jsp

4.1 The Survey-Based Methodology in Comparative Social Research ... 35

Of the five most cited political scientists on earth according to *Google Scholar Profiles* (https://scholar.google.com/citations?view_op=search_authors&hl=en&mauthors=label:political_science), no less than two have advanced research on the topic of the *World Values Survey*, first and foremost the founder and long-time president of the WVS, Professor Ronald F. Inglehart (1934–2021), who passed away on 8 May 2021, and who brought it to an incredible 133,021 citations in *Google Scholar*. Pippa Norris, Professor of Political Science at Harvard University, also belongs to this "royal class" of international political science, and she brought it to 81,954 citations.[1]

For the entire government machinery of a developed country, but also for civil society, the media and the established religious communities and their ecumenism and good coexistence, the data that can be accessed online and without further large statistical programme packages, however, offer undreamed-of possibilities. The "magic link" for this is the address of the online analysis of the *World Values Survey* https://www.worldvaluessurvey.org/WVSOnline.jsp.

The data of the *World Values Survey*—also in the last survey wave 2017 to 2020—always have something new in store for all those who go through life with a mind open to surprises, up to and including data—if anyone is interested—on the acceptance of fare evasion.

There is a rich and evolving debate in the international social sciences about the conclusions that can be drawn from these "omnibus surveys". For some years, some leading economists have also been interested in studying global comparative opinion data, especially from the *World Values Survey* (Alesina & Giuliano, 2015; Alesina et al., 2015). The economic profession's interest in the relationship between religion and economic growth was certainly a contributing factor to the rise of the methodological approach we share with many other social scientists in this study, including Harvard economist Barro (2003) and McCleary and Barro (2006). Prejudice, according to Harvard economist Alberto Alesina, who died all too soon on 23 May 2020, is the antithesis of social trust, which is crucial to long-term economic success. Racism, anti-Semitism, religious intolerance and xenophobia are therefore antithesis to societal trust. The majority of major economic studies using *World Values Survey* data concluded that trust is an important factor for long-term economic growth (Alesina & Giuliano, 2015; Alesina et al., 2015; Zak & Knack, 2001). Trust is also an important factor for the political stability of a nation. Some of the countries

---

[1] For Austrian political science, insofar as it speaks out in the media in Austria, there is, in the author's view, a certain need to catch up here. Austrian political science—to the extent that it has expressed itself on the topics of Islam, Islamism, *political Islam*, etc., in its flagship journal Österreichische Zeitschrift für Politikwissenschaft, ÖZP—still has an unfortunately very limited view of things here over long stretches. Of the articles in question according to Scopus Abdou (2017); Berghahn (2008); Bischof et al. (2008); Dolezal et al. (2008); Hafez (2016); Harrer (2012); Heiss and Feichtinger (2009); Hollomey (2008); Khorchide (2008); Kübel et al. (2008); Liebhart (2015); Mattes (2017); Teshome and Negash (2008); Troy (2015), only Poppenberg and Schlipphak (2016); and Semenov (2016), the analytical tools of the "World Values Survey" or the "Arab Barometer", and only Khorchide (2008); and Poppenborg and Schlipphak (2016) use the term "Islamism" there. Inglehart's and Norris' groundbreaking studies on opinion profiles in West and East, North and South, are unfortunately a "terra incognita australis" for Austrian political discussion.

with very high rates of anti-Semitism, religious and xenophobia, such as Iraq, are also countries with extreme problems of political stability and very low levels of interpersonal trust (Tausch, 2016b; Tausch et al., 2014).

In this publication, social values are analysed within the framework of what is known in political science as the *"civic culture" of the* respective societies (Almond & Verba, 1963; Inglehart, 1988; Silver & Dowley, 2000; cf. also Tausch & Moaddel, 2009).

Sociologists working with the unique comparative and longitudinal opinion survey data from the *World Values Survey have* found, among other things, that there are fairly constant and long-term patterns of value change (Inglehart, 2006; Inglehart & Norris, 2003; Norris & Inglehart, 2012). Inglehart and his colleagues strongly believe that in the West, the ability of representatives of the Roman Catholic hierarchy, still the most numerous Christian denomination, to tell people how to live their lives is steadily declining (see also Morel, 2003).

In our publication, we use the latest edition of the *World Values Survey, 2017–2020*, based on 79 countries and 127,358 interviews. For political science, entering the terrain of studying *political Islam in the* Arab world and in Europe means many methodological problems. Since there are no Eurobarometer surveys yet on the political attitudes of the main confessional groups in Europe, and of course no Eurobarometer survey on the attitudes of Muslims in Europe, our study has to be based on the data of comparative public opinion surveys from publicly available sources. With appropriate multivariate statistical computer software, our analyses based on open-source data should be accessible worldwide at any time.

Items of particular interest for the practical work of global civil societies for the 2017–2020 wave of the *World Values Survey* can be found on the *World Values Survey* website: https://www.worldvaluessurvey.org/wvs.jsp.

4.2 The Design of the Study

First of all, we will now get to know the *Arab Barometer* Project. *"Political Islam"* is simply indispensable to contemporary Middle East studies (Akbarzadeh, 2020; Volpi, 2011). Prominent Arab researchers teaching at Princeton, New Jersey; Amman, Jordan; and Qatar University in Qatar, such as Amaney Jamal,[2] Darwish Al-Emadi[3] and Musa Shteiwi,[4] as lead scholars of the *"Arab Barometer"* project explicitly use the term *"political Islam" in* the questionnaire with five interview items. This measurement and thus the definition of *"political Islam"* is exactly our perspective, and we adopt this perspective without "ifs" and "buts" and 1:1. We strictly adhere here to the machine-readable version of the file as it can be downloaded from the Arab Barometer Consortium in SPSS format.

---

[2] https://scholar.google.com/citations?hl=en&user=CqNmnVwAAAAJ&view_op=list_works.

[3] https://scholar.google.com/scholar?hl=en&as_sdt=0%2C5&q=Darwish+Al-Emadi+&btnG=.

[4] https://scholar.google.com/citations?hl=en&user=jw3SvkQAAAAJ.

4.2 The Design of the Study

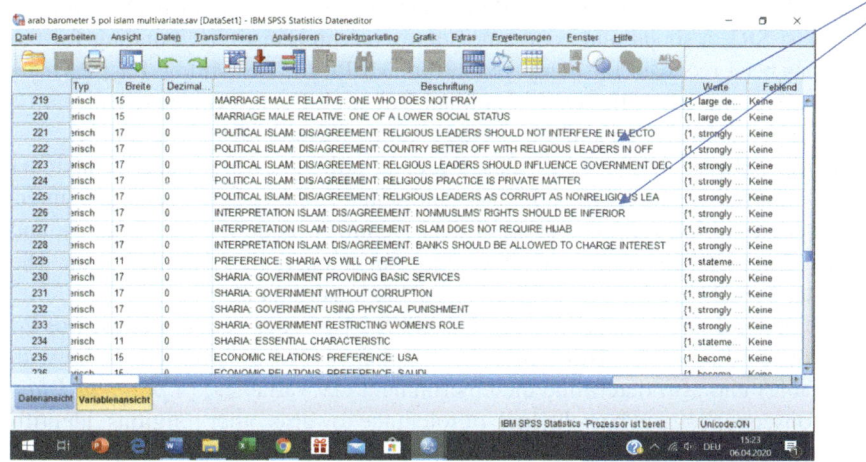

Fig. 4.2 *"Political Islam"* in our *Arab Barometer* IBM-SPSS Data File

According to the Arab Barometer team, *"political Islam"* occurs whenever the following opinions are held in the region:

- It is better for religious leaders to hold public office
- Religious leaders should influence government decisions
- Religious leaders are less corrupt than civilian ones
- Religious leaders should influence elections
- Religious practice is not a private matter.

A direct screenshot from the IBM SPSS file, which is distributed worldwide by the *Arab Barometer Consortium,* provides absolute clarity. The five variables are described by the Arab Barometer as a direct measure of *"political Islam"*; other variables in the analysis are also included in our multivariate analysis (Fig. 4.2).

In addition, the Arab Barometer, co-designed by Qatar University, also includes dimensions of *"political Islam"* in the areas:

- Economy
- Hatred of the West
- Patriarchy
- Rejection of liberal democracy and the rule of law
- Religious intolerance.

This openly available survey data allow researchers to directly access the original data for multivariate analysis (Arab Barometer III–V). The Arab Barometer Wave I was collected in 2007, Wave II, in 2011, Wave III, in 2013, Wave IV, in 2016 and Wave V, in 2018. For many years, participating institutions included the Center for Strategic Studies at the University of Jordan, the Center for Policy Studies at the University of

Michigan, the Palestinian Center for Policy and Survey Research, Princeton University, and SESRI, a social and economic survey research institute. Funding for the project has been received for many years from MEPI, the US Middle East Partnership Initiative, the BBC, the Qatar National Research Fund, Princeton University, the University of Michigan and the United Nations Development Programme.

The Arab Barometer seeks to measure civic attitudes, values and behaviours related to pluralism, freedom, tolerance and equal opportunity; social and interpersonal trust; social, religious and political identities; notions of governance and understandings of democracy; and civic engagement and political participation. The V wave data used here became publicly available in autumn 2019.

The empirical analyses based on IBM-SPSS-24 promax factor analyses of 24 variables according to the *Arab Barometer,* explicitly measure *political Islam* with five variables and also determine the environment (19 variables) of *political Islam* and its consequences, such as the lack of tolerance towards other religions, identification with states that today clearly represent *political Islam,* such as the regime in Iran, President Erdogan in Turkey, restrictive gender norms as defined by the UNDP Human Development Report, 2019, the belief that Muslims should enjoy greater rights in a state than non-Muslims, the negative fixation against the USA, UK and Israel in world politics, the call for a *Sharia* that explicitly introduces corporal punishment and restricts women's rights, and expressing a sympathetic understanding of acts of anti-American terror in the Middle East.

Twenty-four indicators, then, according to our reading, which is based on both our own previous empirical analyses on the topic and the studies cited here by Cammett et al. (2020), Cesari (2021), Driessen (2018), Kucinskas, and Van Der Does (2017), Rahbarqazi and Mahmoudoghli (2020), Tessler (2010), and Wegner and Cavatorta (2019), measure Islamism, while five indicators, No. 13 to No. 17, explicitly measure *political Islam* proper, according to the Arab Barometer:

- Against the marriage of a female relative: one who does not pray.
- Against neighbours: different denominations in Islam.
- Against neighbours: other religion.
- Banks should not be allowed to charge interest.
- Economic relations: Preference: Iran.
- Economic relations: Preference: Qatar.
- Economic relations: Preference: Turkey.
- Biggest threat: Stability: USA, GREAT BRITAIN, ISR.
- Biggest threat: well-being: USA, UK, ISR.
- Islam requires the hijab.
- Men are better at political leadership.
- The rights of non-Muslims should be inferior.
- *Political Islam*: Consent: The country is better off with religious leaders in office.
- *Political Islam*: Consent: Religious leaders should influence government decisions.
- *Political Islam*: Religious leaders are not as corrupt as non-religious leaders.
- *Political Islam*: Religious leaders should interfere in elections.

- *Political Islam*: The practice of religion is not a private matter.
- President Erdogan (very) good.
- Sharia: Government restricts the role of women.
- Sharia: Government with corporal punishment.
- Higher education is more important for men
- Violence against the USA is a logical consequence of interference in the region.
- A woman cannot become prime minister/president.
- Women do not have the same right to divorce.

For some years now, opinion polls such as the *Arab Opinion Index* and the *Arab Barometer Survey have played* an increasing role in the region, documenting three main trends: a desire for democracy, a certain distance from actors such as Iran and Turkey, a more tolerant view of the relationship between religion and the state, and a more distanced and initially rational view of Israel's role in the region. Today, 65% of all Arabs already believe that no religious authority ever has the right to declare followers of other religions infidels. This is an optimistic and important perspective to take into account in times of cultural conflict. The Arab Barometer has long served academic journals such as *The Lancet* and *Political Research Quarterly* as an important source of public health research and social science analysis.

The empirical-analytical starting point for our analyses is, as already mentioned, the important study by Harvard professor Cammett et al. (2020), which also explicitly deals with *political Islam* and political values in the Arab world using data from the Arab *Barometer. The* empirical analyses by Cammett et al. (2020) use longitudinal data from the Arab Barometer as well as data from the *World Values Survey* 2015.

Although the individual studies reviewed here diverge in details, they all agree that organisations such as the Muslim Brotherhood and Hamas can rightly be described as "*political Islam*".

The study thus empirically records *political Islam* strictly according to those criteria explicitly mentioned in the *Arab Barometer*, the most important Arab opinion research project in the world today.

4.3 The Quantitative-Statistical Methodology

Our research attempt is, of course, guided by the great traditions of mathematical-statistical analysis in opinion survey research (Abdi, 2003; Basilevsky, 2009; Braithwaite & Law, 1985; Brenner, 2016; Browne, 2001; Davidov et al., 2008; Dunlap & York, 2008; Fabrigar et al., 1999; Hanson, 2014; Hedges & Olkin, 2014; Inglehart & Norris, 2003, 2012, 2016; Inglehart & Welzel, 2003, 2009; Inglehart & Baker, 2000; Inglehart, 1988, 2006; Kim, 2010; Kimelman, 2004; Kline, 2014; Knippenberg, 2015; Manuel et al., 2006; McDonald, 2014; Minkov & Hofstede, 2011, 2013; Minkov, 2014; Mulaik, 2009; Norris & Inglehart, 2002, 2012, 2015; Suhr, 2012; Yeşilada & Noordijk, 2010).

Our methodological approach lies within a more general framework to study global values using the methodology of comparative and opinion poll-based political science (Brenner, 2016; Hanson, 2014; Knippenberg, 2015; Manuel et al., 2006; Norris & Inglehart, 2015). Our method for assessing global public opinion from global surveys is also based on recent advances in mathematical-statistical factor analysis (Basilevsky, 2009; Cattell, 2012; Hedges & Olkin, 2014; Kline, 2014; McDonald, 2014; Mulaik, 2009; Tausch et al., 2014). Such procedures make it possible to project the underlying structures of the relationships between variables.

Current social science methodology makes it clear that besides factor analysis, other powerful tools of multivariate analysis are available to test complex relationships between an independent variable and independent variables (Blalock, 1972; Tabachnik & Fidell, 2001). In our case, we used standard OLS multiple regression analysis and partial correlation analysis.

4.4 The Multivariate Methods

Our main statistical calculations relied on simple cross-tabulations, comparisons of means, bivariate and partial correlation analyses, factor analyses (promax factor analyses) and standard multiple regressions (OLS) (for a presentation of these methods in international comparative values research, see also Tausch et al., 2014).

With regard to factor analysis and the so-called skewed rotation of factors underlying the correlation matrix, we also refer to important literature on this topic (Abdi, 2003; Browne, 2001; Dunlap & York, 2008; Kim, 2010). The IBM-SPSS routine chosen in this context (IBM-SPSS 24) was the so-called promax rotation of factors (Braithwaite & Law, 1985; Browne, 2001; Fabrigar et al., 1999; Minkov, 2014; Suhr, 2012; Yeşilada & Noordijk, 2010), which in many cases is considered the best rotation of factors in the context of our current research. Put in simple everyday language, the mathematical procedures of rotating factors that best represent the underlying dimensions of a correlation matrix are necessary to make the structure simpler and more reliable.

The problem that factor analysis solves can be described as follows: Can the variables under consideration be represented in mathematically reduced dimensions, and what percentage of the total reality is thus reproduced, and how are these dimensions related to each other? And what is the relationship of the underlying variables to these dimensions? Is there indeed a "factor" or "dimension" such as religiosity and how does this affect phenomena such as "trust in the police" or "anti-Semitism"? Furthermore, is there such a thing as "feminism" and also such a thing as "class" or "status", which influences "trust in the police" or "anti-Semitism" independently of the other "factors"? Promax factor analysis is an established multivariate and mathematical variant among the general techniques of factor analysis that extracts the underlying dimensions from the correlation matrix between variables and precisely answers the questions raised above. It has been extensively described in the literature (Finch, 2006; Tausch et al., 2014, see also Gorsuch, 1983; Harman, 1976; Rummel,

1970; further Finch, 2006; Ciftci, 2010, 2012, 2013; Ciftci & Bernick, 2013). Factor analysis—in our case promax factor analysis—also allows researchers to use the mathematical model to develop a new measurement scale for the new dimensions derived in the research process (Tausch et al., 2014). In modern social indicator research, such new scales are called "parametric indices". The weighting of these indices is done via their eigenvalues (Tausch et al., 2014).

4.5 The Error Margins

For the calculation of the maximum range of variation in the representative opinion poll, the reader is referred to the easy-to-read introduction to the ranges of variation in opinion polls produced by the Cornell University Roper Center (2017). Readers who are more interested in the details are also referred to Langer Research Associates (n.d). Based on the methodological literature on opinion polls, this website provides a direct fluctuation range calculator for opinion polls. It is important to remember that, for example, if the distrust rate of the police in a given country is, say, 5%, the maximum margin of variation for samples of around 1,000 representative interviewees for each country would be $+-1.4\%$. For a mistrust rate of 10%, the range is $+-1.9\%$. For a distrust rate of 15%, the range of variation is $+-2.2\%$ see Langer Research Associates (n.d). That the ranges of variation differ according to the reported distrust of the police is an important fact of opinion survey research theory that is often forgotten to be mentioned in the public debate.

In accordance with standard traditions of empirical opinion research (Tausch et al., 2014), a minimum sample size of at least 30 respondents per country had to be available for all groups and subgroups analysed (Clauß & Ebner, 1970) (Table 4.1).

4.6 Traceability

As mentioned above, this publication is based on the statistical analysis of open survey data and aggregated statistical country data and is based on the commonly used statistical software IBM-SPSS XXIV, which is used at many universities and research centres. The programme contains the full range of modern multivariate statistics, and researchers should be able to arrive at the same results as here if he or she uses the same open data and IBM-SPSS. Our analysis clearly offers only a first attempt and is understood as an invitation to further research, especially by generation, region and gender.

Global value studies are made possible by the availability of systematic and comparative opinion surveys over time under the auspices of leaders in the social science research community, which provide the global population with a questionnaire that has remained relatively constant for several decades.

Table 4.1 Maximum ranges of variation for survey results (the probability of error is 5%)

Sample size	Maximum fluctuation ranges (+−) (%)	Maximum fluctuation ranges (+−) (%)	Maximum fluctuation ranges (+−) (%)	Maximum fluctuation ranges (+−) (%)	Maximum fluctuation ranges (+−) (%)
N	10 or 90	20 or 80	30 or 70	40 or 60	50
20	13.1	17.5	20.1	21.5	21.9
30	10.7	14.3	16.4	17.5	17.9
40	9.3	12.4	14.2	15.2	15.5
50	8.3	11.1	12.7	13.6	13.9
75	6.8	9.1	10.4	11.1	11.3
100	5.9	7.8	9.0	9.6	9.8
250	3.7	5.0	5.7	6.1	6.2
500	2.6	3.5	4.0	4.3	4.4
1.000	1.9	2.5	2.8	3.0	3.1
2.000	1.3	1.8	2.0	2.1	2.2

4.6.1 Arab Barometer

As mentioned above, the sources of our opinion data, which are mentioned in order of appearance in this publication, are the *Arab Barometer* and the *World Values Survey*.

We present valid country values, the population-weighted results for the whole region and our aggregated non-parametric and parametric indicators. The population data used in our work were based on the following sources:

1. https://en.wikipedia.org/wiki/List_of_Arab_countries_by_population
2. https://www.cia.gov/library/publications/the-world-factbook/
3. https://www.worldometers.info/world-population/state-of-palestine-population/

We also mention the future migration potential from Arab countries to Western Europe as well as data on the Islamist attitudes of these potential migrants based on the IBM-SPSS XXIV analysis of Arab barometer data.

For reasons of comprehensibility of the results, we also mention that in the IBM-SPSS files provided free of charge by the *Arab Barometer,* the missing values and the non-respondents unfortunately have to be eliminated "manually" in a multivariate analysis. For example, the variable Q201B_12, Trust Islamist Movement, is scaled from 1.00 "*great trust*" to 4.00 "*no trust*". 98.00 is the "*don't know*" and 99.00 is the "*refused*". If I correlate this variable, for example, with the variable Q606_1: POLITICAL ISLAM: DIS/AGREEMENT: RELIGIOUS LEADERS SHOULD NOT INTERFERE IN ELECTIONS, which is coded in the same way as the variable "Trust Islamist Movement", I must take this into account in the calculation and first eliminate the answers with the values "98" and "99" with the IBM-SPSS routine "*Select cases*" *in order* to only then obtain a valid correlation. Otherwise, the programme would calculate the values 1, 2, 3, 4 as well as 98 and 99.

4.6.2 The Files of the World Values Survey

The data from the *World Values Survey were taken* from Haerpfer et al. (2020). This data covered the period 2017–2020 and include 79 countries and territories. For comparison purposes, we also refer to the analyses "*World Values Survey_Longitudinal_1981_2014_spss_v2015_04_18*.sav" and "*World Values Survey_Longitudinal_1981_2016_Spss_v20180912*.sav" used in previous publications by the author. Our analyses thus cover a large number of countries around the world (more than 73% of the world's population). In the case of the *World Values Survey, as* with the *Arab Barometer*, the original data have been made freely available to the global scientific public and allow for a systematic, multivariate analysis of opinion structures based on the original anonymous interview data. There is a huge literature on the analysis of such reliable and regularly repeated global opinion surveys at the world level (cf. Davidov et al., 2008; Inglehart, 2006; Norris & Inglehart, 2015; Tausch et al., 2014).

4.7 Macro-quantitative Country Data

In the second part of our study, in which we analyse data from the *World Values Survey* to measure religiously motivated political extremism (RMPE), we also use *World Values Survey data* to calculate multivariate analyses with aggregated country data. The freely accessible "*master file*" of the author's recent macro-quantitative analyses is the electronic publication:

- Tausch (2019) [Migration from the Muslim world to the West: Its most recent trends and effects. Jewish Political Studies Review, 30(1–2), 65–225, available at http://jcpa.org/article/migration-from-the-muslim-world-to-the-west-its-most-recent-trends-and-effects/ (with data definitions and sources). Free data download available from https://www.academia.edu/37568941/Migration_from_the_Muslim_World_to_the_West_Its_Most_Recent_Trends_and_Effects]

Further data for free download can be found at:

- https://uibk.academia.edu/ArnoTausch/Documentation-for-books-and-articles

    there in particular:

- https://www.academia.edu/49256828/Aggregate_Data_Excel_File_for_the_Study_Political_Islam_and_Religiously_Motivated_Political_Extremism_RMPE_in_the_Arab_World_and_Austria_in_International_Comparison_Findings_from_the_Arab_Barometer_and_World_Value_Survey_Data

This file documents all 300 variables used and is in EXCEL format.

Open Access This chapter is licensed under the terms of the Creative Commons Attribution 4.0 International License (http://creativecommons.org/licenses/by/4.0/), which permits use, sharing, adaptation, distribution and reproduction in any medium or format, as long as you give appropriate credit to the original author(s) and the source, provide a link to the Creative Commons license and indicate if changes were made.

The images or other third party material in this chapter are included in the chapter's Creative Commons license, unless indicated otherwise in a credit line to the material. If material is not included in the chapter's Creative Commons license and your intended use is not permitted by statutory regulation or exceeds the permitted use, you will need to obtain permission directly from the copyright holder.

Chapter 5
The Empirical Results of Our Empirical Study

Abstract The study clearly shows that identification with Turkey and Iran, with a political Islam that also influences elections and results in a theocracy, promotes religious and gender discrimination and advocates an Islamist interpretation of Islam, are very much the most important, interrelated syndromes of political Islam, which together explain more than 50% of the total variance of the 24 model variables used. If the states of Europe want to win the fight against jihadism, they must work closely with the moderate Arab states, such as Egypt, Jordan, Morocco, Saudi Arabia, the United Arab Emirates and other Arab Gulf states, and be aware that, on a population-weighted basis, 41% of all Arabs now view the Muslim Brotherhood, which is the strongest and most coherent force in political Islam today, negatively or very negatively. According to the data brought to light here, only 7% of people in the Arab world now have a high level of trust in their country's Islamist movement, while 14% have some trust, 19% have little trust, but 60% have no trust. Our overall index—Overcoming political Islam shows that Morocco and Tunisia are the top performers, while Iraq and Sudan bring up the rear. Following an important study by Falco and Rotondi (2016), we also explore the question of whether political Islam is more prevalent or less prevalent among the more than 20% of the Arab population who plan to emigrate in the coming years than among the population as a whole. Far from feeding alarmist horror scenarios, our evaluation shows firstly that Falco and Rotondi (2016) are correct in their thesis that among potential migrants to the West, political Islam is certainly less pronounced than among the Arab population as a whole. On a population-weighted basis, only 13.11% of potential migrants to the West openly state that they trust the country-specific Islamist movement. In the second part of our empirical evaluations, we explore religiously motivated political extremism (RMPE) by international comparison on the basis of the following items of the World Values Survey, which are sparse but nevertheless available on this topic: The proportion of the global population who favour religious authorities in interpreting the law while accepting political violence is alarmingly high in various parts of the world and is raising fears of numerous conflicts in the coming years in an increasingly unstable world system. It amounts to more than half of the adult population in Tajikistan (the international record holder), and Malaysia and some non-Muslim-majority countries. In many countries, including NATO and

EU member states, it is an alarming 25–50%, and we mention here the Muslim-majority countries Iraq, Lebanon, Bangladesh, Kazakhstan, Nigeria and Indonesia. It is 15–25% even in core countries of the Western security architecture, but also in the Muslim-majority countries: Pakistan, Iran and Tunisia. Only in the best-ranked countries, among them the Muslim-majority countries Albania, Egypt, Bosnia and Herzegovina, Kyrgyzstan, Azerbaijan and Jordan, the potentially fatal combination of mixing religion and law and accepting political violence has a relatively small following of less than 15%. In the sense of the theses of the late Harvard economist Alberto Alesina (1957–2020), social trust is an essential general production factor of any social order, and the institutions of national security of the democratic West would do well to make good use of this capital of trust that also exists among Muslims living in the West.

Keywords Political Islam · Religiously motivated political extremism · Arab Barometer · World Values Survey · Opinion surveys in the Arab world · Empirical political science research · Middle East research · Promax factor analysis · Global opinion surveys · Migration · Terrorism

We now present our results in a condensed form. We emphasise that anyone with access to the Internet and the IBM-SPSS statistical software package should be able to arrive at the same results as we did.

5.1 Results on Political Islam According to the Arab Barometer

Table 5.1 shows how strongly the Arab public already distances itself from the Islamist movements in the region. Only in Yemen is the strong trust in the Islamist movement in double figures. The selection of which Islamist movement it is in each case was made by the Arab Barometer Consortium and cannot be determined from the machine-readable data set.

Table 5.2 shows the support rates for Islamism and *political Islam* in the region on a population-weighted basis. Indeed, such weighting is very important in real terms, since, for example, opinion in Egypt, with its huge population, carries much more weight for the entire Arab world than, say, that of Lebanon or the West Bank and Gaza, with their relatively small populations.

If people throughout the Arab world were allowed to vote freely in a referendum, the following rules, opinions and regulations would each receive an absolute majority:

- Against a woman who marries a man who does not pray
- Terrorism against the USA is a logical consequence of US interference in the region

5.1 Results on Political Islam According to the Arab Barometer

Table 5.1 Trust in Islamist movements in the Arab world

	Trust: Islamist movement				
	Great confidence	Some confidence	Little trust	No trust	N (valid answers)
Libya	1.7	7.6	10.2	80.4	864
Iraq	4.1	10.3	13.9	71.7	1037
Egypt	5.7	8.4	14.5	71.4	1160
Tunisia	4.6	14.1	13.3	68.0	1091
Jordan	4.0	13.6	15.7	66.7	1015
Total	6.4	15.5	18.4	59.7	9278
West Bank + Gaza	6.5	17.0	19.8	56.7	1125
Morocco	9.4	22.8	20.9	46.9	979
Sudan	9.8	18.0	27.0	45.2	840
Yemen	11.1	26.2	30.1	32.6	1167

- Men are the better political leaders
- The USA, UK and Israel pose the greatest threat to the stability and well-being of the region
- Banks should not be allowed to charge interest

More than a third of the Arab population supports the following claims:

- Turkish President Erdogan is (very) good
- Islam requires women to wear the hijab
- Preference for closer economic relations with Turkey
- The country would be better off if religious leaders were in office
- For a Sharia that uses corporal punishment
- Religious practice is not a private matter
- Preference for stronger economic relations with Qatar
- A woman cannot become prime minister/president
- In society, the rights of non-Muslims should be secondary
- Religious leaders[1] should influence government decisions
- Rejection of neighbours who belong to a different religion
- Sharia should limit the role of women
- Religious leaders are not as corrupt as non-religious leaders.

Only the following positions are genuine minority positions, supported by less than 1/3 of the total Arab population surveyed:

---

[1] The gender-neutral asterisk notation, so popular in continental Europe, could and should be omitted here. Islamists will have no interest in putting women or *LBGT communities* in leadership positions; and imprisonment and the death penalty for lesbians and homosexuals are the order of the day in countries like Iran, cf. https://www.dw.com/en/the-difficulties-of-being-gay-in-iran/a-56717484.

Table 5.2 Islamism and *political Islam* in the Arab MENA countries

	% of the total Arab population
Economic relations: preferred: Iran	22.1
Higher education is more important for men	23.7
Political Islam: religious leaders should interfere in elections	23.8
Women do not have the same right to divorce	31.5
Political Islam: religious leaders not as corrupt as non-religious leaders	33.1
Against neighbours: different denominations in Islam	33.6
Sharia: government restricts the role of women	34.9
Political Islam: agreement: religious leaders should influence government decisions	35.8
Against neighbours: other religion	35.8
The rights of non-muslims should be inferior	37.3
Woman cannot become prime minister/president	38.8
Economic relations: preference: Qatar	40.6
Political Islam: religious practice is not a private matter	41.4
Sharia: government uses corporal punishment	44.2
Political Islam: agreement: country better off with religious leaders in office	45.0
Economic relations: preference: turkey	46.8
Islam requires the hijab	47.4
President Erdogan (very) good	49.5
Biggest threat: wellbeing USA, great Britain, ISR	52.7
Banks should not be allowed to charge interest	53.8
Biggest threat: stability USA, UK, ISR	53.9
Men are better at political leadership	69.3
Violence against us logical consequence of interference in the region	70.1
Against the marriage of a female relative: one who does not pray	76.2

- Preference for closer economic relations with Iran
- Religious leaders should interfere in elections
- Higher education is more important for men than for women
- Women do not have the same right to decide to divorce.

Table 5.3 now analyses the population-weighted profiles of *political Islam* among migrants in the region, broken down by migration destination. Potential migrants to Western countries identify around 20–40% with destinations that the *Arab Barometer* describes as *political Islam,* but nowhere are adherents of *political Islam* an absolute majority of potential migrants in the West. While Table 5.3 shows the total values per

5.1 Results on Political Islam According to the Arab Barometer

migration destination, Table 5.7 shows the individual country values per migration destination.

Table 5.4 shows the aggregated country results. We mark each result above 1/3 of the support rates for Islamism / *political Islam*. Our data are the first true estimate of *political Islam* in the Arab world:

Table 5.3 *Political Islam* among those willing to migrate and in the Arab population as a whole according to the Arab *Barometer*

Sample/subsample	"Political Islam"	Total (population weighted)
Immigrants to the Gulf region	Country better off with religious leaders in office	43.77
Immigrants to the West	Country better off with religious leaders in office	33.65
Arab countries in total	Country better off with religious leaders in office	45.03
Immigrants to the Gulf region	Religious leaders should influence government decisions	36.30
Immigrants to the West	Religious leaders should influence government decisions	29.39
Arab countries in total	Religious leaders should influence government decisions	35.80
Immigrants to the Gulf region	Religious leaders are not as corrupt as non-religious leaders	29.88
Immigrants to the West	Religious leaders are not as corrupt as non-religious leaders	26.35
Total Arab countries	Religious leaders are not as corrupt as non-religious leaders	33.05
Immigrants to the Gulf region	Religious leaders should interfere in elections	21.66
Immigrants to the West	Religious leaders should interfere in elections	21.91
Arab countries in total	Religious leaders should interfere in elections	23.85
Immigrants to the Gulf region	Religious practice is not a private matter	41.24
Immigrants to the West	Religious practice is not a private matter	38.41
Total Arab countries	Religious practice is not a private matter	41.39

Table 5.4 Political Islam in the Arab world according to the Arab Barometer (only valid percentages were evaluated)

	Algeria	Egypt	Iraq	Jordan	Lebanon	Libya	Morocco	West Bank + Gaza	Sudan	Tunisia	Yemen
Political Islam: religious leaders should interfere in elections	37.3	8.8	24.4	27.0	27.6	28.5	26.1	23.2	29.0	24.7	40.4
Political Islam: agreement: country better off with religious leaders in office	48.7	46.6	33.3	39.3	16.9	27.4	46.3	35.4	67.0	27.5	38.6
Political Islam: agreement: religious leaders should influence government decisions	45.7	22.0	49.3	35.1	20.8	33.0	26.6	33.7	55.1	25.1	43.6
Political Islam: religious practice is not a private matter	55.2	27.8	24.1	54.3	21.0	39.3	56.5	57.3	54.9	28.9	54.3
Political Islam: religious leaders not as corrupt as non-religious leaders	40.4	33.7	28.2	26.9	34.2	30.7	28.7	28.0	32.9	31.0	37.0
The rights of non-Muslims should be inferior	41.8	33.0	22.5	23.6	20.7	36.9	29.1	26.8	51.5	27.6	70.7
Islam requires the hijab	37.3	62.3	52.2	52.7	26.2	47.0	42.5	61.1	26.0	10.2	57.8
Banks should not be allowed to charge interest	74.3	31.8	67.0	81.7	60.4	79.7	46.1	73.3	50.2	61.7	71.7
Sharia: government uses corporal punishment	44.3	42.7	21.8	43.9	31.4	33.8	44.1	33.0	58.5	20.0	76.0
Sharia: government restricts the role of women	30.9	34.5	34.9	27.5	27.4	35.4	37.7	23.7	35.7	23.6	48.2
Economic relations: preference: Qatar	38.8	16.0	30.9	76.9	47.0	10.2	54.1	56.2	76.6	51.9	55.9

(continued)

5.1 Results on Political Islam According to the Arab Barometer

Table 5.4 (continued)

	Algeria	Egypt	Iraq	Jordan	Lebanon	Libya	Morocco	West Bank + Gaza	Sudan	Tunisia	Yemen
Economic relations: preference: Turkey	54.5	15.9	48.1	82.6	44.0	31.4	59.8	73.8	75.3	64.4	60.8
Economic relations: preferred: Iran	22.3	9.4	34.8	27.5	38.2	16.2	20.0	38.2	34.4	38.8	18.7
Woman cannot become prime minister/president	61.5	34.0	32.1	39.4	21.1	44.7	19.8	34.6	49.3	31.4	47.2
Men are better at political leadership	73.0	73.1	72.8	74.7	49.6	71.3	42.0	66.3	83.3	57.1	70.8
Higher education is more important for men	21.8	27.4	21.1	16.9	10.1	16.4	15.9	13.5	29.1	20.9	30.9
Women do not have the same right to divorce	29.7	32.3	18.9	21.0	12.5	25.6	24.8	18.9	51.8	18.3	46.0
Against neighbours: other religion	32.6	40.6	21.4	18.2	22.4	55.7	36.1	30.7	34.0	28.4	55.2
Against neighbours: different denominations in Islam	34.4	46.0	16.3	35.7	3.2	46.7	39.9	31.3	23.9	23.8	26.7
Against the marriage of a female relative: one who does not pray	80.1	82.4	62.9	63.0	45.6	81.6	61.4	66.7	93.6	25.4	95.1
Violence against us logical consequence of interference in the region	68.3	76.5	61.7	68.7	80.1	57.6	52.8	78.4	77.3	47.6	84.1
President Erdogan (very) good	72.0	17.4	41.6	83.6	30.8	23.1	65.5	72.2	81.4	69.4	55.3
Biggest threat: stability USA, Great Britain, ISR	38.8	60.3	53.2	60.4	84.6	48.4	44.2	89.2	65.3	49.0	39.6
Biggest threat: wellbeing Usa, Great Britain, ISR	39.1	59.7	50.6	58.3	83.3	44.2	42.0	91.0	64.5	39.1	41.0

5.2 Political Islam and Migration Potential According to the Arab Barometer

The Gallup Institute has conducted serious surveys on global migration patterns.[2] The surveys were based on representative interviews with 259,542 people over the age of 15 in 135 countries for the period 2007–2009. The countries selected to represent 93% of the world's population in this age group.

Gallup said at the time:

> The United States is the most popular destination for the 700 million adults who want to move permanently to another country. Nearly a quarter (24%) of these respondents, or more than 165 million adults worldwide, name the United States as their future residence. With another estimated 45 million saying they would like to move to Canada, North America is one of the top two most desired regions. The remaining top desired countries (where an estimated 25 million or more adults would like to go) are predominantly European countries. Forty-five million adults who would like to move name the United Kingdom or France as their desired destination, while 35 million would like to move to Spain and 25 million would like to move to Germany. Thirty million name Saudi Arabia and 25 million Australia. About 210 million adults around the world would like to move to a European Union country, which is the same as the estimated number who would like to move to North America. However, about half of the estimated 80 million adults living in the EU who would like to move permanently to another country would like to move to another country within the EU - the highest desired intra-regional migration rate in the world.

In a brief paragraph, Gallup provided an important key to evaluating other surveys, particularly for the roughly 630 million adults worldwide who intend to move to another country. Less than one-tenth of them—about 48 million adults—say they plan to make that move in the next 12 months.[3] Again, less than half of those who plan to move—about 19 million adults—take the necessary steps such as applying for a visa or residence permit and buying tickets for the trip. With a little simple arithmetic, we can say that out of 100 people who said in the Gallup poll that they wanted to emigrate, only 3.0 will actually emigrate. This radical interpretation of the data, which excludes any alarmism, goes back to Faßmann and Hintermann (1997), Faßmann and Münz (1994), who were correct in their migration forecast for Eastern Europe, which defined as the final migration potential those who really wanted to emigrate in the next year, and thus in the great EU enlargement of 2004. Gallup said at the time in the original sound bite:

> Of the approximately 630 million adults worldwide who want to move to another country, less than one-tenth of them - about 48 million adults - have told Gallup they plan to move in the next 12 months. Less than half of those planning to move - about 19 million adults - have taken the necessary steps, such as applying for visas or residence permits and buying tickets.[4]

Table 5.5 is the first result of the rough estimate of the total, general migration potential from the Arab world:

---

[2] https://news.gallup.com/poll/124028/700-million-worldwide-desire-migrate-permanently.aspx.
[3] https://news.gallup.com/poll/152951/Nearly-Million-Worldwide-Planning-Migrate-Soon.aspx.
[4] https://news.gallup.com/poll/152951/nearly-million-worldwide-planning-migrate-soon.aspx.

5.2 Political Islam and Migration Potential According to the Arab Barometer

Table 5.5 Desire to emigrate to Western countries, in % of the total Arab population according to the Arab *Barometer*

The aim of migration	Algeria	Egypt	Iraq	Jordan	Lebanon	Libya	Morocco	Palestine	Sudan	Tunisia	Yemen
USA	12.683	13.100	6.480	24.434	15.468	6.481	7.729	12.439	15.976	1.687	8.772
Canada	29.106	9.825	3.685	20.701	25.899	10.185	23.028	12.111	9.822	10.123	4.873
UK	9.431	0.655	3.177	2.149	5.755	4.938	1.735	2.455	1.183	5.215	0.585
France	33.659	7.860	3.558	1.018	12.950	4.938	30.599	2.291	11.953	26.687	1.170
Germany	21.301	6.769	16.773	5.69	11.871	8.642	24.132	8.183	3.787	9.816	4.288
Spain	18.374	1.747	2.033	1.018	1.619	1.852	21.136	0.491	1.538	1.227	0.195
Italy	16.911	10.917	2.033	1.810	2.878	16.667	21.136	2.291	3.432	11.963	0.975

Table 5.6 Trust in the Islamist movement of the respective home country as a percentage of the total Arab population and as a percentage of the Arab population willing to emigrate to the West

	Trust: Islamist movement		Trust: Islamist movement	
	Total population	N	Migrants in the West	N
Egypt	14.14	1199	8.41	108
Iraq	14.37	1203	5.19	179
Jordan	17.64	1186	17.50	224
Libya	9.38	950	12.63	102
Morocco	32.18	1209	17.80	363
Palestine	23.47	1281	12.41	160
Sudan	27.74	896	20.00	205
Tunisia	18.70	1192	10.10	213
Yemen	37.36	1203	23.53	69
Population weighted sum	21.46		13.11	

Table 5.6 provides information on the confidence of the population in the Arab countries in the country-specific Islamist movement according to the *Arab Barometer* Survey. It clearly shows that those who are willing to migrate to the West have less confidence in the country-specific Islamist movement than the total Arab population of the respective country. On a population-weighted basis, 13.11% of potential migrants to the West openly state that they trust the country-specific Islamist movement. Realistically, therefore, we can expect the immediate influx of a six-figure number of Islamist movement supporters in France, Canada, Germany and the USA, while the influx of Islamist movement supporters to Italy, Spain and the UK is likely to be in the five-figure range.

Table 5.7 shows the support rates for Islamism and *political Islam* in the region on a population-weighted basis for those willing to migrate to the West and for the total population of the respective Arab country. Table 5.3 analyses the population-weighted profiles of *political Islam* among those willing to migrate in the region, broken down by migration destination. While Table 5.3 shows the total values per migration destination, Table 5.7 now shows the individual country values per migration destination, as announced earlier.

Here, too, it can be seen that Falco and Rotondi (2016), were correct in their assumption that the proportion of those who support radical Islamist positions is lower among those willing to emigrate (to Western countries) than in the population as a whole.

5.2 Political Islam and Migration Potential According to the Arab Barometer

Table 5.7 Support for *political Islam* (five items according to the Arab Barometer survey) as a percentage of the total Arab population willing to emigrate to the West and as a percentage of the total Arab population

		Algeria	Egypt	Iraq	Jordan	Lebanon	Libya	Morocco	Palestine	Sudan	Tunisia	Yemen
Immigrants to the West	Religious leaders should interfere in elections	37.02	9.60	17.78	25.49	23.27	27.32	14.54	24.59	36.13	22.07	33.33
Immigrants to the West	Country better off with religious leaders in office	48.43	28.65	23.98	35.53	20.10	28.43	23.99	21.38	58.21	23.92	29.84
Immigrants to the West	Religious leaders should influence government decisions	44.71	16.33	40.99	34.00	20.00	33.50	10.91	28.57	45.27	25.92	38.71
Immigrants to the West	Religious practice is not a private matter	56.15	27.41	15.41	50.55	19.51	47.47	40.89	44.59	53.05	30.82	56.91
Immigrants to the West	Religious leaders are not as corrupt as non-religious leaders	30.95	27.72	19.01	22.47	25.00	23.59	15.74	19.34	32.55	24.94	34.45
Immigrants to the West	N *Arab Barometer*	687	200	351	464	411	207	745	310	399	458	126
Arab countries in total	Religious leaders should interfere in elections	37.32	8.80	24.40	27.01	27.59	28.47	26.13	23.16	29.04	24.66	40.43
Arab countries in total	Country better off with religious leaders in office	48.68	46.62	33.32	39.25	16.88	27.36	46.32	35.36	67.02	27.52	38.58
Arab countries in total	Religious leaders should influence government decisions	45.73	21.97	49.25	35.09	20.78	33.05	26.64	33.73	55.15	25.14	43.59
Arab countries in total	Religious practice is not a private matter	55.19	27.78	24.09	54.34	20.98	39.27	56.51	57.31	54.88	28.91	54.32
Arab countries in total	Religious leaders are not as corrupt as non-religious leaders	40.37	33.67	28.20	26.91	34.17	30.68	28.66	28.02	32.86	31.01	37.02
Arab countries in total	N *Arab Barometer*	2332	2400	2458	2400	2400	1962	2400	2493	1758	2400	2399

5.3 Towards a Multivariate Analysis of Political Islam and Migration

Let us now briefly describe our multivariate analysis of the variables measuring *political Islam*, based on the promax factor analysis using the IBM-SPSS XXIV computer programme with the Arab Barometer data. We propose to name the resulting promax factors based on the factor loadings > 0.500 (structural matrix) as follows. The number of factors results from the application of the classical eigenvalue criterion > 1.0 for multivariate statistics.

- Distance to Turkey and Iran
- Distance from *political Islam*—interference in elections
- Against the theocracy
- Against religious discrimination
- Against discrimination based on gender
- Against an Islamist interpretation of Islam.

The model explains 50.1% of the total variance (Table 5.8).

Table 5.9 then shows the results for potential migrants in Western countries. Potential migrants in Spain and Italy are least likely to sympathise with *political Islam*, while potential migrants in the USA and Canada hold views that are more influenced by the patterns of *political Islam*.

The highest factor loadings of the opinion "*Violence against the United States of America is a logical consequence of (US) interference in the region*", which is a clear indicator of support for anti-American terrorism, are statistically explained by the factor "*Islamist interpretation of Islam*" (factor loading: 0.512) as well as by the factor "*Preference for Turkey and Iran*" (factor loading: 0.347).

Resilience to anti-American terrorism in the Arab world is consistent with the following statements:

- ECONOMIC RELATIONS: NONE PREFERENCE: IRAN
- ECONOMIC RELATIONS: NONE PREFERENCE: QATAR
- ECONOMIC RELATIONS: NONE PREFERENCE: TURKEY
- INTERPRETATION OF ISLAMS: BANKS SHOULD CHARGE INTEREST
- INTERPRETATION OF ISLAM: ISLAM DOES NOT PRESCRIBE THE HIJAB
- INTERPRETATION OF ISLAM: THE RIGHTS OF NON-MUSLIMS MUST NOT BE INFERIOR
- NEGATIVE OPINION: PRESIDENT ERDOGAN.

5.3.1 Conclusions and Perspectives from the Arab Barometer Data

On the one hand, our analysis has shown sufficiently clearly that Falco and Rotondi (2016), were right when they said that Islamist radicalism among potential migrants from the Arab world to the West is lower than in the population as a whole. However, as this radicalism is still large enough to pose a serious security problem, we were able to show in the study for *Directions in Terrorism* that from 1979 to 2019, no less than 755 people died in Islamist terrorist attacks in Europe. Our quantitative analysis in this regard in Tausch (2021), based on data from Science Po, provided clear evidence of an 11-year cycle of Islamist terrorist activity in Europe, based on an econometric time series analysis. Based on our prediction using the quantitative, proven techniques of statistical spectral analysis and cross-correlations (Tausch, 2021), we will—with all the caution that is required in such predictions based on spectral analysis and cross-correlations—see another peak of Islamist terrorism in Western Europe in 2026/2027.

Our multivariate promax factor analysis, based on nineteen items from the Arab Barometer survey and explaining more than 50% of the total variance, has shown that support for Turkey under Erdogan and Iran under his regime are the most important streams of *political Islam* today. This factor alone explains 14.3% of the variance.

Our analyses have broadly confirmed those perspectives on "political Islam" already elaborated in full detail in Solomon (2016), Solomon and Tausch (2020a, 2020b, 2021a, 2021b). Our conclusions—for reasons of space—only briefly refer to this literature here, and we only note here that there are major differences in the degree of support for political Islam as to which population willing to migrate it is in the Arab world. The migrants who express a preference for the destination countries of Spain and Italy identify least with political Islam, while the population who would prefer to go to the USA and Canada identify most strongly with political Islam.

5.4 Results of the World Values Survey on Religiously Motivated Political Extremism (RMPE) in Europe Compared to 79 Countries in the World

In the following, we will use the *World Values Survey to* estimate religiously motivated political extremism (RMPE) in Europe compared to 79 countries worldwide. The two questions we will evaluate in this context based on the *World Values Survey are:*

> Many things are desirable, but not all are necessary components of a democracy. For each of the following things, please tell me to what extent you consider it a necessary component of a democracy. Use this scale, with 1 being "not at all a necessary component of a democracy" and 10 being "a necessary component of a democracy". Religious leaders ultimately determine the interpretation of the laws.
>
> For each of the following, can you please tell me whether you think it is okay under no circumstances, all circumstances or anything in between? Please use the following scale. Politically motivated violence

Our findings thus provide a limited insight into the landscape of religiously motivated political extremism (RMPE) in Europe. Due to the unfortunately very small possible sample size of Muslims in the omnibus survey of the *World Values Survey* for Europe, our results for this population group are only in the nature of informed indications, also emphasising that even with better samples, the international comparative results are unlikely to change.

According to Table 5.10, based on the data of the *World Values Survey*, a certain or greater degree of religiously motivated political extremism (RMPE) is found in 9.7% of the total population in Austria and in 16.4% of Muslims in Austria. It should be **noted** that the results in Table 5.10, must also be compared with the ranges of variation. Austria's Muslims are ahead of the total population in Portugal, the USA, France, the UK, Lithuania, Spain and Slovakia, to name but a few countries.

47.3% of Muslims in Austria are against political violence and against a religious role in legislation. 23.6% are against political violence but can imagine a religious role in legislation. 12.7% are secular and accordingly against a religious role in legislation, but accept political violence. Our empirical definition of RMPE fully applies to 16.4%.

Austria—total population

	Against political violence	For political violence	Total
Against the role of religion in legislation	62.9	9.0	71.9
For the religious role in legislation	18.4	9.7	28.1
Total	81.4	18.6	100.0

$N = 1561$; the RMPE value outlined in red has a range of variation of $\pm\ 1.4\%$ with a probability of error of 5%

62.9% of the total population in Austria are against political violence and against a religious role in legislation. 18.4% are against political violence but can imagine a religious role in legislation. 9.0% are again secular and thus against a religious role in legislation, but accept political violence. Our empirical definition of RMPE fully applies to 9.7%.

The proportion of people who favour religious authorities in interpreting the law while accepting political violence is alarmingly high in various parts of the world, raising fears of numerous conflicts in the years to come in an increasingly unstable world system. It amounts to more than half of the adult population in Tajikistan (the international record holder), the Philippines, Vietnam, South Korea and Malaysia. In many countries, including NATO and EU member states, it is an alarming 25–50%: Iraq, Macau SAR, Lebanon, Slovakia, Hong Kong SAR, Thailand, Bangladesh, Mexico, Chile, Ukraine, Russia, Bolivia, Ecuador, Spain, Kazakhstan, Lithuania, Guatemala, Nigeria and Indonesia. It is 15–25% in the following states, including core countries of the Western security architecture: UK, Taiwan ROC, France, Netherlands, Belarus, Argentina, USA, Nicaragua, Peru, Montenegro, Pakistan, Iran, Colombia, Armenia, Tunisia, Portugal, Czech Republic, Poland and Italy. Only the best-ranked countries Albania, Ethiopia, Iceland, Macedonia, Egypt, Andorra, Germany, Puerto Rico, Cyprus, Bosnia and Herzegovina,

5.4 Results of the World Values Survey on Religiously Motivated Political ...

Croatia, Denmark, Japan, Estonia, Bulgaria, Austria, Australia, Norway, Slovenia, Kyrgyzstan, Hungary, Sweden, Azerbaijan, Finland, Zimbabwe, Serbia, Jordan, Georgia, Switzerland, New Zealand, Burma, Greece, China, Brazil and Romania, the potentially fatal combination of mixing religion and law and accepting political violence has a relatively small following of less than 15%.

Table 5.11 is our final table of the empirical comparison of RMPE in 79 countries around the world.

The following charts show the reality of religiously motivated political extremism (RMPE) in the global system across all geographical and denominational boundaries. Our maps, as well as the data from the *World Values Survey, are* designed to soften rigid and ideologically entrenched fronts. We refer our readers to subsequent studies on our maps:

- Figure 5.1 Acceptance of political violence shows that it is not the Arab region, and certainly not the Arab region as a whole, that is to be identified with the acceptance of political violence; Southeast Asia as well as Iraq and Spain, on the other hand, are real problem zones. In Europe, the Nordic states, the Federal Republic of Germany and, fortunately, Hungary as well as the countries of the Balkan region are relatively little affected by the acceptance of political violence.
- Electronic Appendix Figure 2: Standard Deviation—Acceptance of Political Violence uses this important statistical indicator to show the extent to which the fringes of the political system are already radicalised and reject a consensus of non-violence. This statement applies not only to Spain and Serbia, but also to France and large parts of America, the former Soviet Union and West Asia.
- Electronic Appendix Figure 3: The Depth of the Problem of Country Residents Endorsing political violence now organises the data underlying Fig. 5.2 in a more graphically appealing form. The red-coloured zones of the global scale for acceptance of political violence are thought-provoking; however, the analysis should also take into account that in most countries of the Arab world for which data are available, performance on this indicator is even better than in the core countries of Western democracies.
- Figure 5.2 The map "*Religious authorities should interpret the laws*" shows that the approval of this sentence, which runs counter to everything a modern secular state stands for in the sense of Hans Kelsen's "*pure doctrine of law*" (Hans Kelsen, 1881–1973; cf. Kelsen, 2005, posthumously) and in the sense of the Enlightenment, is geographically very similar to the maps of political and social values described by Ronald F. Inglehart in his extensive work as "*survival values versus self-development values*" and "*traditional values versus secular-rational values*".[5]
- The combination of the two RMPE measures (Electronic Appendix Figure 4: % in favour of political violence + interpretation of laws by religious authorities; Electronic Appendix Figure 5: Depth of the problem of residents of a country who endorse political violence + interpretation of laws by religious authorities;

---

[5] https://www.worldvaluessurvey.org/WVSNewsShow.jsp?ID=428.

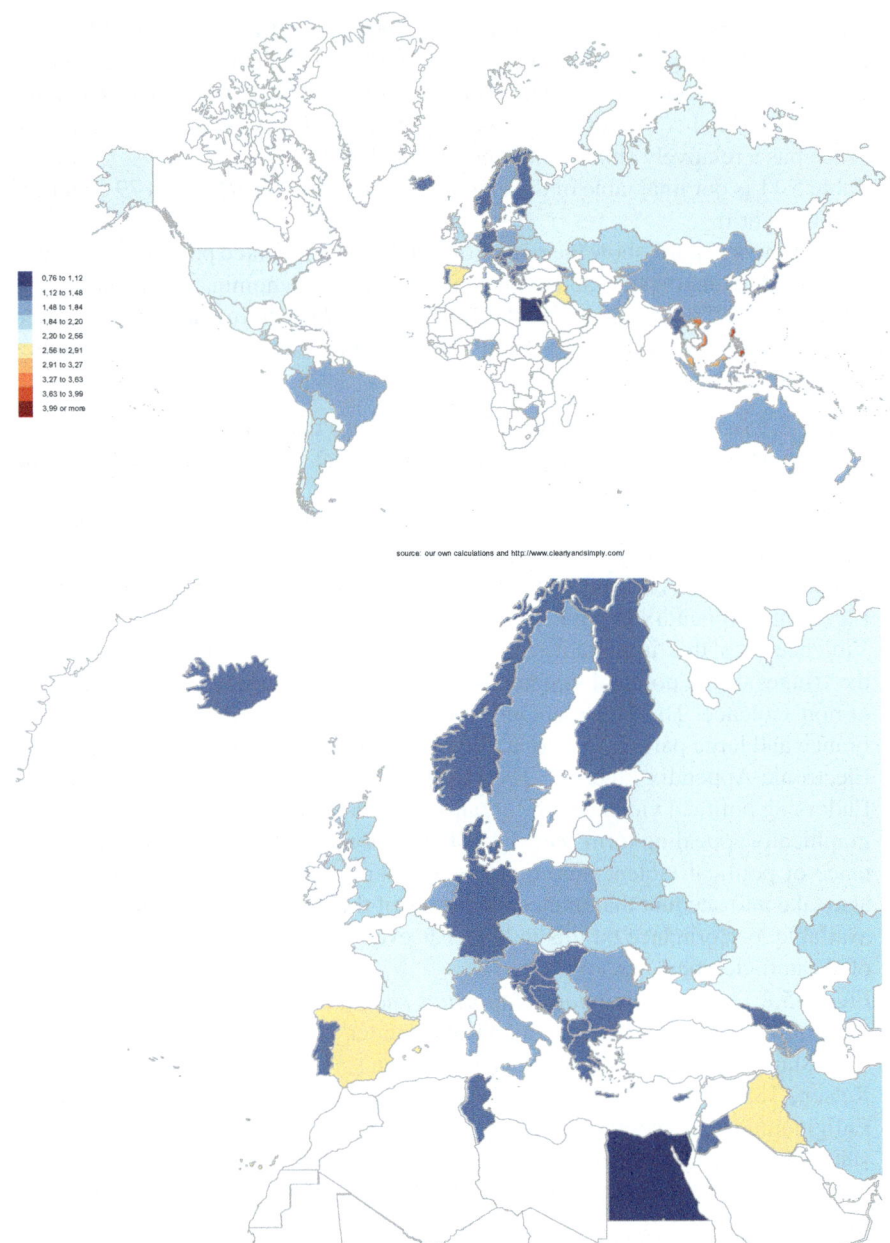

Fig. 5.1 Acceptance of political violence

5.4 Results of the World Values Survey on Religiously Motivated Political ...

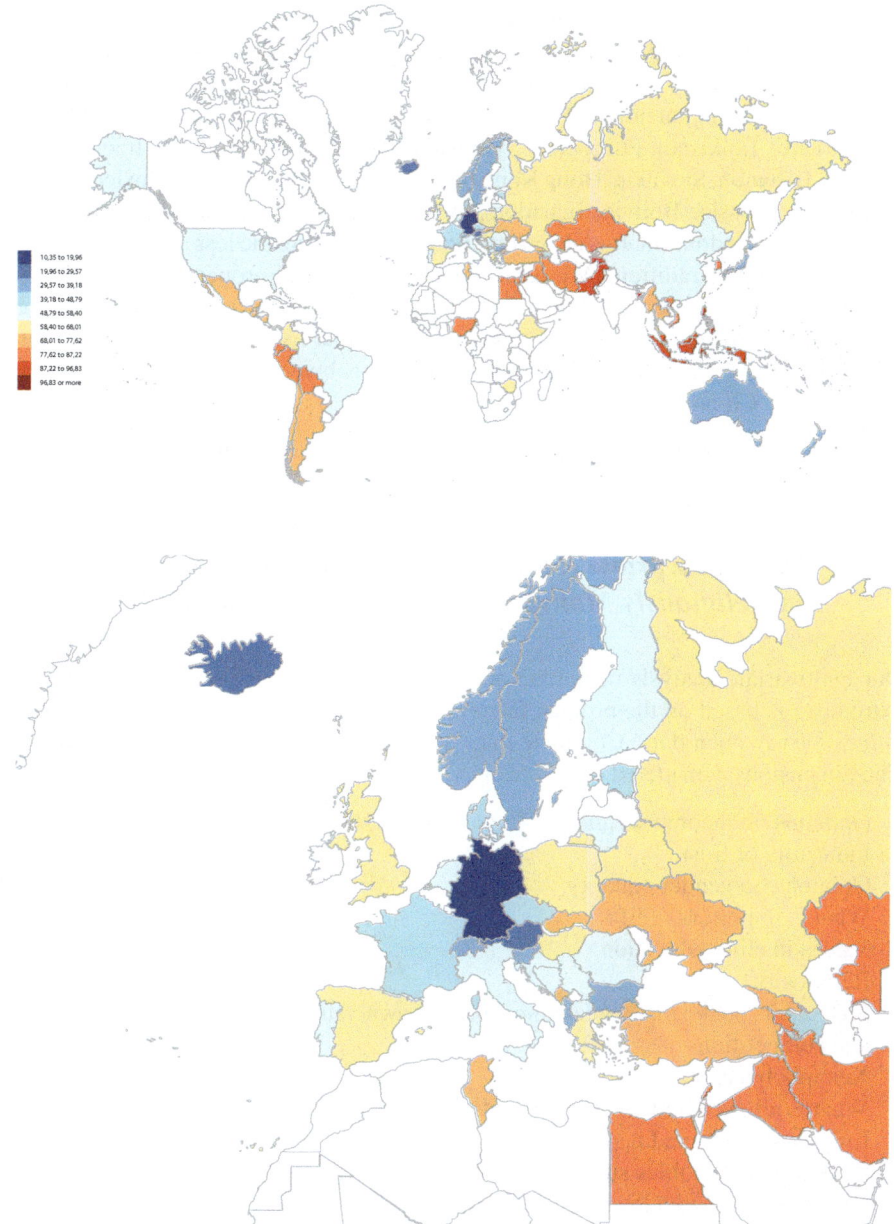

Fig. 5.2 Religious authorities should interpret the laws

and Electronic Appendix Figure 6: Radicalisation of the "anti-Kelsen camp" (% of population who affirm interpretation of laws by religious authorities endorse political violence)) yields an interesting difference in perspective from Inglehart and Welzel's map mentioned earlier. The real problem cases of RMPE (RMPE > 25%) are: Tajikistan, Philippines, Vietnam, South Korea, Malaysia, Iraq, Macau SAR, Lebanon, Slovakia, Hong Kong SAR, Thailand, Bangladesh, Mexico, Chile, Ukraine, Russia, Bolivia, Ecuador, Spain, Kazakhstan, Lithuania, Guatemala, Nigeria and Indonesia. It is also worth noting that among the less developed countries outside the traditional Western democracies and the European Union with less than 15% RMPE are the following countries whose good performance allows for optimistic prospects: Albania, Ethiopia, Macedonia, Egypt, Puerto Rico, Bosnia and Herzegovina, Kyrgyzstan, Azerbaijan, Zimbabwe, Serbia, Jordan, Georgia, Myanmar, China and Brazil.

Following these remarks, we now present our successive charts:

5.4.1 The Multivariate Results of the World Values Survey on Religiously Motivated Political Extremism (RMPE)

Our multivariate analysis of the factors influencing religiously motivated political extremism is based on the promax factor analysis statistical model using the *World Values Survey* open data. Complete data were available for 74 states in the world. The dimensions considered were:

- Opinions on income inequality
- Indicators of trust
- Opinions on gender equality
- What is important in life
- Values in child education
- Religiosity
- Statements on the market economy, private ownership of the means of production and competition
- Xenophobia and racism
- What is allowed and what is forbidden?
- Life satisfaction and happiness
- Background variables such as gender, age
- Dissatisfaction with the political system
- What constitutes a democracy (redistribution of income by the state, separation of state and religion).

For reasons of comprehensibility of our investigation, we name the variables used in the model after the original English text:

1. We need greater income inequality
2. one cannot be careful enough (lack of trust)

5.4 Results of the World Values Survey on Religiously Motivated Political ...

3. No confidence: Judiciary/courts
4. not important in life: Family
5. University is equally important for boys and girls
6. No trust: The police
7. Important characteristics of the child: Obedience
8. Important qualities in children: Sense of responsibility
9. Gender: female
10. Men are not better leaders than women
11. not important in life: Religion
12. Harmful competition
13. Never attend church services
14. not important in life: Politics
15. Important qualities in children: Determination and perseverance
16. Justified: Someone who accepts a bribe
17. Rejecting neighbours: People of a different race
18. Justified: Political violence
19. Justified: Homosexuality
20. How important is God in your life?
21. Rejecting neighbours: Immigrants/foreign workers
22. Important qualities in children: Imagination
23. Feeling of unhappiness
24. Important characteristics of the child: religious faith
25. Satisfaction with one's own life
26. not important in life: Work
27. Rejecting neighbours: Homosexual
28. Important qualities in children: Tolerance and respect for other people
29. Private vs. state ownership of companies
30. Age
31. Dissatisfaction with the political system
32. Democracy: Religious authorities interpret the laws
33. Democracy: Governments tax the rich and subsidise the poor.

Our factor analytic model, which extracts 12 factors, explains more than 58% of the variance of the variables. Again, it should be noted that the number of factors extracted results from the simple and rigorous application of the mathematical-statistical criterion of eigenvalue > 1.0, which is still the standard of multivariate factor analysis today.

1. Secularism
2. Feminism
3. Political marginalisation
4. Racism and xenophobia
5. Corruption and lawlessness
6. Happiness
7. Rejection of the Calvinist work ethic
8. Rejection of the neoliberal market economy

9. Unpolitical young generation
10. Education: Responsibility versus obedience
11. Education: Imagination versus tolerance
12. Redistributive state.

Two extracted factors play a prominent role in explaining RMPE: secularism (dampens RMPE) and corruption and lawlessness (promotes RMPE).

The factor loadings of > ± 0.100 on the secularism factor with the variables of the model are
Not important in life: Religion 0.858
   Never attends church services 0.764
   Justified: Homosexuality 0.568
   Men are not better business people than women 0.293
   University is equally important for a boy and a girl 0.275
   not important in life: Work 0.196
   Important child traits: Imagination 0.185
   Important child traits: Determination Perseverance 0.176
   Important characteristics of children: Tolerance and respect for others 0.174
   not important in life: Family 0.130
   Important characteristics of the child: Sense of responsibility 0.124
   Rejected neighbours: people of a different race − 0.106
   No confidence: The police − 0.107
   Private vs. state ownership of companies − 0.128
   We need more income inequality − 0.140
   Gender: female − 0.140
   Important child traits: Obedience − 0.211
   one cannot be careful enough (lack of confidence) − 0.325
   Neighbours reject: Homosexuals − 0.364
   Democracy: Religious authorities interpret the laws − 0.488
   Important characteristics of the child: religious belief − 0.659
   How important is God in your life − 0.828.

The factor loadings of > ± 0.100 on the factor corruption and lawlessness on the variables of the model are
It is justifiable for someone to accept a bribe 0.816
   Justified: Political Violence 0.816
   Justified: Homosexuality 0:308
   Harmful competition 0.207
   Democracy: Religious authorities interpret the laws 0.204
   not important in life: Family 0.109
   Satisfaction with the political system 0.100
   University is equally important for a boy and a girl − 0.128
   Neighbours reject: Homosexuals − 0.151
   Age − 0.231.

5.4 Results of the World Values Survey on Religiously Motivated Political ...

The key variable of the RMPE, Democracy: Religious authorities interpret the laws, is explained by the factors of the model as follows (factor loadings of > ± 0.100)
Redistributive state 0.401
   Unpolitical young generation 0.369
   Rejection of the neoliberal market economy 0.276
   Corruption and lawlessness 0.204
   Racism and xenophobia 0.145
   Rejection of the Calvinist work ethic − 0.208
   Feminism − 0.393
   Secularism − 0.488.

The second key variable of the RMPE, Justifiable: political violence, is explained by the factors of the model as follows (factor loadings of > ± 0.100)
Corruption and lawlessness 0.816.

The correlations of the components of secularism (> ± 0.100) were
Feminism 0.425
   Rejection of the Calvinist work ethic 0.302
   Happiness 0.103
   Racism and xenophobia − 0.255
   Rejection of the neoliberal market economy − 0.256
   Unpolitical young generation − 0.412.

The correlation components of corruption and lawlessness (> ± 0.100) were
Rejection of the neoliberal market economy 0.139
   Education: Imagination versus tolerance 0.131
   Education: responsibility versus obedience − 0.165.

Readers interested in social science are recommended to read the following factor-analytical tables, which also document the factor scores at the country level (Electronic Appendix Table 8 through to Electronic Appendix Table 11).

5.4.2 The Extent and Global Drivers of Acceptance of Political Violence and Religiously Motivated Political Extremism (RMPE)—Multivariate Analysis of World Values Survey Data at the Global Level

In the above multivariate analysis of the *World Values Survey* interview data at the level of globally interviewed individuals, it was found first and foremost that the RMPE cannot be separated from the climate of lawlessness that many observers consider rampant, especially in the Western industrialised countries, and secondly that the drivers of the key RMPE variables (democracy: Religious authorities interpret

Table 5.8 Parametric index: overcoming *Political Islam*

	Overall index—overcoming *political Islam*	N
Morocco	1.490	1518
Tunisia	1.214	1971
Algeria	0.708	1766
Libya	0.511	1739
Lebanon	0.226	1171
Egypt	− 0.108	1727
Palestine	− 0.214	2030
Jordan	− 0.461	2108
Yemen	− 0.714	2182
Sudan	− 0.776	1508
Iraq	− 1.204	2273

Table 5.9 Parametric index: overcoming *political Islam* for those wanting to emigrate in the Arab world to the West

The aim of migration	Overall index—overcoming *political Islam*	N
Spain	0.831	305
Italy	0.309	493
France	0.189	808
Western Europe (other)	0.007	170
UK	− 0.016	201
Germany	− 0.032	712
Eastern Europe	− 0.185	309
Canada	− 0.221	898
USA	− 0.483	707

Table 5.10 RMPE in Austria according to the *World Values Survey*

Austria—Muslims			
	Against political violence (%)	For political violence (%)	Total (%)
Against the role of religion in legislation	47.3	12.7	60.0
For the religious role in legislation	23.6	16.4	40.0
Total	70.9	29.1	100.0

Muslim sample $N = 55$; the RMPE value outlined in red has a range of variation of ± 9.4% with a probability of error of 5%

5.4 Results of the World Values Survey on Religiously Motivated Political ...

Table 5.11 RMPE at international level according to the *World Values Survey*

	Proportion of people who favour religious authorities in the interpretation of laws	Proportion of people who favour religious authorities in the interpretation of laws and accept political violence	% Radicalisation of the camp that rejects secular democracy[6]
Albania	38.82	1.40	3.64
Ethiopia	64.78	4.83	7.47
Iceland	28.21	5.28	18.93
Macedonia	50.89	5.31	10.71
Egypt	84.66	5.32	6.43
Andorra	50.05	6.02	12.05
Germany	19.96	6.20	31.48
Puerto Rico	49.41	6.22	12.64
Cyprus	66.60	6.23	20.79
Bosnia and Herzegovina	50.88	7.34	14.46
Croatia	49.14	7.38	15.13
Denmark	40.56	8.23	20.33
Japan	32.55	8.55	27.22
Estonia	47.16	8.76	18.91
Bulgaria	39.05	9.23	24.42
Austria	28.02	9.55	34.40
Australia	33.70	10.35	30.99
Norway	38.47	10.39	27.08
Slovenia	37.88	10.92	28.99
Kyrgyzstan	60.36	11.06	18.94
Hungary	67.62	11.56	17.26
Sweden	30.86	11.81	39.14
Azerbaijan	41.64	12.52	31.23
Finland	51.55	12.98	25.28
Zimbabwe	66.53	12.99	19.57
Serbia	54.07	13.01	24.31
Jordan	85.35	13.03	15.34
Georgia	68.53	13.16	19.31
Switzerland	30.83	13.19	43.78
New Zealand	37.60	13.20	37.93

(continued)

---

[6] % of those who reject the interpretation of laws by religious authorities but consider political violence acceptable.

Table 5.11 (continued)

	Proportion of people who favour religious authorities in the interpretation of laws	Proportion of people who favour religious authorities in the interpretation of laws and accept political violence	% Radicalisation of the camp that rejects secular democracy
Burma	73.58	13.67	18.59
Greece	60.09	13.70	22.84
China	49.31	13.74	27.95
Brazil	49.25	14.25	29.84
Romania	57.77	14.86	26.19
Italy	52.07	15.06	29.25
Poland	61.92	15.22	25.07
Czech Republic	43.40	16.16	38.07
Portugal	58.39	16.52	28.46
Tunisia	70.07	16.98	24.26
Armenia	84.66	17.19	20.48
Colombia	64.34	18.09	28.12
Iran	82.98	19.32	23.85
Pakistan	95.91	19.48	20.87
Montenegro	71.91	20.49	28.66
Peru	82.22	21.40	26.46
Nicaragua	76.00	21.50	28.29
USA	51.12	22.25	43.89
Argentina	76.48	22.51	30.23
Belarus	62.12	22.76	38.02
Netherlands	53.19	23.33	44.12
France	48.07	23.42	49.76
Taiwan ROC	67.16	24.08	35.85
UK	61.38	24.15	39.56
Indonesia	90.88	27.46	30.46
Nigeria	79.30	27.81	35.11
Guatemala	73.81	28.06	38.37
Lithuania	55.95	29.13	54.01
Kazakhstan	83.53	29.94	37.72
Spain	59.28	29.96	51.42
Ecuador	80.84	31.01	38.49
Bolivia	84.86	31.58	37.69
Russia	65.52	32.10	50.98

(continued)

5.4 Results of the World Values Survey on Religiously Motivated Political ...

Table 5.11 (continued)

	Proportion of people who favour religious authorities in the interpretation of laws	Proportion of people who favour religious authorities in the interpretation of laws and accept political violence	% Radicalisation of the camp that rejects secular democracy
Ukraine	69.89	32.43	49.43
Chile	70.09	33.41	48.05
Mexico	73.18	34.40	47.74
Bangladesh	94.58	35.00	37.00
Thailand	75.43	38.10	50.65
Hong Kong SAR	68.72	39.90	58.19
Slovakia	75.13	41.06	55.14
Lebanon	78.83	41.58	52.97
Macau SAR	61.77	42.76	69.33
Iraq	85.50	48.08	56.24
Malaysia	92.73	55.32	59.65
Korea. South	86.10	55.42	64.37
Vietnam	85.73	61.97	72.28
Philippines	91.75	65.00	70.84
Tajikistan	96.83	75.83	78.31
Turkey	72.88		

the laws), are the demand for a redistributive state, the apolitical young generation, the rejection of the neoliberal market economy, corruption and lawlessness, and racism and xenophobia, and that the best blockages against this are rooted in feminism and secularism. This explanation confirms an old empirical finding of the author that in multicultural and multiethnic societies, market mechanisms rather than state governance principles prove to be most effective (Tausch & Prager, 1993); a finding that was specified in Tausch et al. (2014) to the effect that there is a positive affinity between Islam and capitalism (Tausch, 2021).

As sufficiently justified in the methodology of comparative social research, the analysis of international survey data can now also be linked to aggregate data from economics, political science and sociology (cf. Tausch, 2021; Tausch et al., 2014). In the following, we present such an attempt, based on the freely accessible EXCEL data from international standard sources specially prepared for this publication:

- https://www.academia.edu/49256828/Aggregate_Data_Excel_File_for_the_Study_Political_Islam_and_Religiously_Motivated_Political_Extremism_RMPE_in_the_Arab_World_and_Austria_in_International_Comparison_Findings_from_the_Arab_Barometer_and_World_Value_Survey_Data

Table 5.12 Regression-analytical model of the drivers of acceptance of political violence—multivariate analysis of *World Values Survey* data at the global level

Variable	Regression coefficient B	Standard error	Beta	T-value	Sig
(Constant)	1.415	0.122		11.615	0.000
Catholics per total population	0.381	0.160	0.260	2.379	0.020
Followers of Eastern religions per total population	1.912	0.896	0.233	2.134	0.037
Gallup/UNDP survey on satisfaction with the local labour market	0.009	0.004	0.284	2.488	0.016
World Values Survey polls: Rejection of the market economy	0.331	0.160	0.234	2.067	0.043

Adj $R^2 = 27.9\%$; $n = 65$ countries; $F = 7.285$; Error $p = 0.000$

Table 5.12 presents a regression-analytical model of the drivers and barriers to the acceptance of political violence based on the *World Values Survey* data at the international level. The model could be built for 65 countries with complete data. It explains 27.9% of the variance in the acceptance of political violence in adjusted terms and fulfils well the usual criteria of widely used statistical significance tests (listed below the table for statistically interested readers).

When explaining the statements on the acceptance of political violence, which may seem paradoxical to some readers, we have to accept, as stated above, that it is not the Arab region as a whole that can be identified with the acceptance of political violence; **Southeast Asia as well as Iraq and Spain, on the other hand, are real problem zones**. In Europe, the Nordic states, the Federal Republic of Germany and, fortunately, Hungary as well as some countries in the Balkan region are relatively little affected by the social acceptance of political violence. We had also pointed out that the fringes of the political system in many states of the world are already strongly radicalised and reject a consensus of non-violence. This observation applies not only to Spain and Serbia, but also to France and large parts of both Americas, the former Soviet Union and West Asia. In most states of the Arab world for which data are available, the situation is even better than in many core countries of Western democracies.

The sad fact for Western society is that especially in Catholic countries, where the decline of traditional values is particularly rapid, there is a renewed acceptance not only of corruption but also of political violence. This problem also arises in countries with a confessional orientation towards Eastern religions. The rejection of free-market competition *(competition is harmful) is* also clearly associated with a higher acceptance of political violence, according to the *World Values Survey*.

Following Olson (1982), as well as Tausch and Heshmati (2013), Tausch et al. (2014), we identify regional distributional coalitions expressed in satisfaction with

5.4 Results of the World Values Survey on Religiously Motivated Political ...

subnational, i.e. local, labour market policies as further drivers of the acceptance of political violence. At first glance, this may seem completely counterintuitive, even absurd. Yet the 20 countries with the highest satisfaction with local labour markets are Saudi Arabia, Thailand, Kuwait, Oman, Laos, Qatar, the Philippines, Singapore, Paraguay, Tajikistan, Chile, Panama, Turkmenistan, Venezuela, Brazil, Uruguay, Cambodia, Djibouti, Uzbekistan and Norway. Among them are some countries with high political acceptance of violence.

Among the countries with a high level of dissatisfaction with the local labour market, such as Greece, Italy, Serbia, Bosnia and Herzegovina, Croatia, Spain, Bulgaria, Ireland, Moldova, Hungary, Montenegro, Portugal, Macedonia, Slovakia, Romania, Slovenia, the UK, Egypt, Cyprus and the Czech Republic, there are again some states with a low acceptance of political violence.

In future, international social science can discover important causal mechanisms here that can be of great significance for a future of world society without political violence and which are all compatible with the neoliberal explanatory patterns mentioned at the beginning.

Electronic Appendix Figure 7 is the map of the unstandardised residuals of our regression equation from Table 5.12. The relatively high propensity for political violence in the USA, Russia and Spain still forms a statistical outlier.

To further analyse which mechanisms lead to the acceptance of political violence in world society and which mechanisms block it, we also calculated the partial correlations of the acceptance of political violence with the 300 variables of our country aggregate data set,[7] holding constant the level of human development and its square. This idea goes back to Nobel Laureate in Economics Simon Kuznets (1955, 1976), for whom development processes such as social inequality have a curvilinear shape. Inequality increases in the course of industrialisation and only decreases again at a relatively high level of development. This idea has found wide application in the social and economic sciences. On this basis, it has become common today to associate crisis phenomena of a more general nature, and not just inequality, with "Kuznets curves".

The result of the partial correlations is that, also irrespective of the level of development, the population in countries with a certain level of satisfaction is more inclined to political violence, especially also when a higher inequality rate is added (Table 5.13).

In any case, international comparative social science still has to invest a lot of analytical capacity to really fathom the mechanisms of acceptance of political violence.

In Table 5.13, we present our model of the drivers of acceptance of religiously motivated political extremism (RMPE) based on a multivariate multiple regression analysis of *World Values Survey* data at the global level with national aggregate data.

---

[7] https://www.academia.edu/49256828/Aggregate_Data_Excel_File_for_the_Study_Political_Islam_and_Religiously_Motivated_Political_Extremism_RMPE_in_the_Arab_World_and_Austria_in_International_Comparison_Findings_from_the_Arab_Barometer_and_World_Value_Survey_Data.

Table 5.13 Partial correlation of factors influencing acceptance of political violence—multivariate analysis of *World Values Survey* data at the global level (constant: HDI 2018 & (HDI 2018)^2)

	Partial correlation with acceptance of political violence (HDI 2018 & HDI (2018)^2 constant)	Significance (two-sided)	Degree of freedom
Gallup satisfaction survey: local labour market	0.419	0.000	68
Gallup satisfaction poll: efforts to deal with the poor	0.400	0.001	68
WVS: rejection of the neoliberal market economy	0.387	0.001	67
Share of the richest 1% in total income	0.374	0.010	44
WVS: trust in institutions	0.326	0.040	38
Gallup Satisfaction Survey: quality of Education	0.317	0.007	68
Gallup satisfaction poll: trust in national government	0.314	0.009	66
WVS: female rejection of market economy and democracy	0.312	0.039	42
Gallup satisfaction survey: standard of Living	0.309	0.009	68
Annual growth rate of international migration, 1960–2005	0.302	0.028	51
Gallup satisfaction survey: job	0.293	0.014	68
Overcoming the gender gap in health and survival	0.290	0.019	63
UNDP GSN physical integrity	0.287	0.041	49
Share of Chinese immigrants in total immigrants	0.285	0.014	71
Distance to Belgium	0.270	0.026	66
Happy planet index. HPI	0.268	0.027	66
Chinese immigrants per 1 million total population	0.268	0.022	71

(continued)

5.4 Results of the World Values Survey on Religiously Motivated Political … 73

Table 5.13 (continued)

	Partial correlation with acceptance of political violence (HDI 2018 & HDI $(2018)^2$ constant)	Significance (two-sided)	Degree of freedom
Gallup satisfaction survey: quality of health care	0.267	0.026	68
Prison population per 100,000	0.251	0.034	70
Global migration senders 2017	0.250	0.033	71
Gallup satisfaction survey: Overall Life Satisfaction Index	0.249	0.037	68
Coefficient of human inequality 2013	0.248	0.044	64
Current account balance 2021 per GDP	0.247	0.036	70
Government consumption expenditure	− 0.240	0.049	66
Social protection (ILO)	− 0.249	0.042	65
Foreign saving rate	− 0.281	0.021	65
WVS: tolerance and respect + post-materialism	− 0.297	0.050	42
EU recipients of global migration from this country in %, 2017	− 0.303	0.009	71
Doctors (per 1000 persons), 2010	− 0.305	0.012	65
Migration to the EU in per thousand of the total population, 2010	− 0.339	0.005	66
WVS: overall civil society index	− 0.345	0.029	38
WVS: mistrust of the army and the press	− 0.346	0.021	42
Unemployment rate	− 0.390	0.001	63
Absolute latitude	− 0.426	0.001	58
WVS: the law-abiding society	− 0.664	0.000	38

Adj. $R^2 = 50.3\%$; $N = 63$; $F = 6.304$; Error $p = 0.000$

The regression model explains 50.3% of the variance of the RMPE for 63 states with complete data with good joint significance values of the whole equation.

The main drivers of acceptance of religiously motivated political extremism (RMPE) that are significant at the 5% level are, in this order

- Workers' remittances as % of GDP
- Global migration sending countries 2017
- Gallup Satisfaction Survey: Local Labour Market
- Gallup Satisfaction Survey: Quality of Education.

The main obstacles to a high acceptance of religiously motivated political extremism (RMPE) are

- Proportion of Muslims in the total population
- Gallup satisfaction poll: Freedom of choice
- Proportion of Orthodox Christians in the total population
- Gallup Satisfaction Survey: Overall Life Satisfaction Index.

Electronic Appendix Table 11 shows the predicted RMPE, the actual RMPE values and the residuals based on the regression-analytical model of the drivers of religiously motivated political extremism in the multivariate analysis of the *World Values* Survey data at the global level in Table 5.14. The 15 states whose structural conditions suggest that RMPE may increase rapidly in the near future are Kyrgyzstan, Germany, Nicaragua, Croatia, Albania, Hungary, Norway, Italy, Egypt, Estonia, Switzerland, Portugal, New Zealand, Poland and Bangladesh.

The 15 countries whose structural conditions suggest that weighty forces are at work that could flatten the RMPE are South Korea, Spain, Malaysia, Nigeria, Vietnam, Slovakia, Chile, the Netherlands, Tunisia, Tajikistan, Lebanon, Ukraine, France, the UK and the Philippines. Electronic Appendix Figure 8 illustrates the data in Electronic Appendix Table 12 in an analytical map.

Table 5.14 Regression-analytical model of the drivers of acceptance of religiously motivated political extremism—multivariate analysis of *World Values Survey* data at the global level

	Regression coefficient B	Standard error	Beta	T	Significance
(Constant)	126.203	99.758		1.265	0.212
Workers' remittances as % of GDP	0.843	0.258	0.406	3.275	0.002
Proportion of orthodox Christians in the total population	−20.781	8.589	−0.310	−2.420	0.019

(continued)

5.4 Results of the World Values Survey on Religiously Motivated Political ...

Table 5.14 (continued)

	Regression coefficient B	Standard error	Beta	T	Significance
Proportion of Muslims in the total population	− 24.147	7.803	− 0.489	− 3.095	0.003
Gallup satisfaction survey: quality of education	0.454	0.185	0.362	2.449	0.018
Gallup satisfaction survey: freedom of choice	− 0.517	0.186	− 0.535	− 2.775	0.008
Gallup satisfaction survey: local labour market	0.343	0.129	0.374	2.659	0.010
Gallup satisfaction survey: overall life satisfaction index	− 6.643	3.276	− 0.436	− 2.028	0.048
Gallup satisfaction survey: safety	− 0.244	0.143	− 0.221	− 1.703	0.095
Gallup satisfaction poll: trust in national government	0.240	0.121	0.305	1.990	0.052
Global migration senders 2017	0.000	0.000	0.306	3.158	0.003
HDI 2018	− 225.931	237.972	− 1.487	− 0.949	0.347
HDI (2018)^2	180.241	160.141	1.859	1.126	0.266

Open Access This chapter is licensed under the terms of the Creative Commons Attribution 4.0 International License (http://creativecommons.org/licenses/by/4.0/), which permits use, sharing, adaptation, distribution and reproduction in any medium or format, as long as you give appropriate credit to the original author(s) and the source, provide a link to the Creative Commons license and indicate if changes were made.

The images or other third party material in this chapter are included in the chapter's Creative Commons license, unless indicated otherwise in a credit line to the material. If material is not included in the chapter's Creative Commons license and your intended use is not permitted by statutory regulation or exceeds the permitted use, you will need to obtain permission directly from the copyright holder.

Chapter 6
Discussion and Conclusions of This Study in the Context of the Empirical Results Obtained

Abstract We have emphasised in this chapter that our findings do not fit into any simple political template of thinking that has existed for many years on the topic of "Islam" and "migration". Our findings show that surveys authoritatively designed by Arab social science clearly measure "political Islam", but that the phenomenon is less pronounced in the population that says it wants to emigrate to the West than in the Arab population as a whole. We have also clearly pointed out that the RMPE cannot be separated from the climate of lawlessness that many observers unfortunately now see rampant, especially in Western industrialised countries, and secondly, that the drivers of the key variables of the RMPE are rooted in such patterns of thought and values as the demand for a redistributive state, the apolitical young generation, the rejection of the neoliberal market economy, corruption and lawlessness as well as racism and xenophobia. The best blockades against the RMPE are feminism and secularism. An honest examination of the phenomenon of RMPE will also not be able to ignore the fact that especially in Catholic countries, where the decay of traditional values is progressing particularly fast, not only the acceptance of corruption but also of political violence is on the rise again. This problem also arises in countries with a confessional orientation towards Eastern religions. The rejection of free-market competition (competition is harmful) is also clearly linked to a higher acceptance of political violence, according to the World Values Survey. The results of our study on political Islam in the Arab world certainly also have some very shocking aspects that cannot simply be swept under the carpet. Weighted by population, the Arab Barometer data show that more than 70% of Arabs have a (sympathetic) understanding of the anti-American terror that culminated in 9/11 in Manhattan. More than 44% of Arabs favour Sharia with corporal punishment, more than 37% want the rights of non-Muslims in society to be less than those of Muslims, and more than 34% also want Sharia to restrict the rights of women. We finally highlight that following the late Harvard economist Alberto Alesina (1957–2020), social trust is an essential general production factor of any social order, and the institutions of national security of the democratic West would do well to make good use of this capital of trust that also exists among Muslims living in the West.

Keywords Political Islam · Religiously motivated political extremism · Arab Barometer · World Values Survey · Opinion surveys in the Arab world · Empirical political science research · Middle East research · Global opinion surveys · Migration · Terrorism · Trust · Alberto Alesina (1957–2020)

In the following, we would like to draw some very preliminary conclusions, if possible, for the sociopolitical debate in Europe.

6.1 Political Islam and Terrorism

Our findings do not fit into any simple political template of thinking that has existed for many years on the topic of "Islam" and "migration". Our findings show that surveys authoritatively designed by Arab social science clearly measure *"political Islam"*, but that the phenomenon is less pronounced in the population that says it wants to emigrate to the West than in the Arab population as a whole. We have also clearly pointed out that the RMPE cannot be separated from the climate of lawlessness that many observers unfortunately now see rampant, especially in Western industrialised countries, and secondly, that the drivers of the key variables of the RMPE are rooted in such patterns of thought and values as the demand for a redistributive state, the apolitical young generation, the rejection of the neoliberal market economy, corruption and lawlessness, as well as racism and xenophobia. The best blockades against the RMPE are feminism and secularism.

An honest examination of the phenomenon of RMPE will also not be able to ignore the fact that especially in Catholic countries, where the decay of traditional values is progressing particularly fast, not only the acceptance of corruption but also of political violence is on the rise again. This problem also arises in countries with a confessional orientation towards Eastern religions.

The rejection of free-market competition (*competition is harmful*) is also clearly linked to a higher acceptance of political violence, according to the *World Values Survey*.

Precisely because our results are based on open, freely accessible data and a good part of the literature we use is already freely accessible via portals such as *"Google Scholar"* or at least easily accessible in our academic libraries, our publication is also an invitation to readers to literally "run hot" their own IT devices, laptops, tablets, even smartphones with the statistical sources and materials used here and their open-access versions. The more there is critical debate on our findings, the better. And for readers of this essay from the security agencies of the Free World, this essay offers an important warning that takes on an unfortunately strong timeliness in the face of such images as the angry crowds that tried to storm the Capitol in Washington on 6 January 2021: freedom is always threatened by politically motivated violence, and misunderstood messages from the world of religions can help to intensify that violence.

This publication thus took readers on a journey into empirical research on *"political Islam"* and religiously motivated political violence. On this journey, it was necessary to leave behind the rigid discussion fronts that have emerged in the West and to adjust to new and surprising insights, but also to new literature from the world's major *peer-reviewed journals*.

Thus, at the end of this study, we are faced with less than satisfactory data, further complicated by the fact that the sample for Muslims in Europe included in the *World Values Survey is* relatively small.

As shown in the methodology chapter of this paper, this unfortunately resulted in rather unfavourable maximum ranges of variation. Thus, to the best of our knowledge and belief, we could only offer a first "keyhole perspective" of the realities for the opinions of Muslims in Europe and in other Muslim "diaspora" states, whereby we must admittedly already note that such comparative studies—based on omnibus surveys of the entire population—still have a certain validity and significance as a *"second best solution"* (cf. Tausch, 2010, 2019; Tausch & Karoui, 2011). Social research in the West would do well to adopt questions from the *World Values Survey*, the *Arab Barometer* and the *PEW Institute in Washington* for samples of Muslims in the West; the same applies to *Eurobarometer, in order* to finally obtain reliable comparative data on the realities of the migration world. If the European Commission in Brussels in particular really takes the declarations on integration and coexistence on our continent seriously, *Eurobarometer* must finally start to collect a valid survey on the life perspectives of the confessional groups in Europe or—in confessionally neutral terms—all those who or whose parents were not born in the EU-27, using the questions of the *World Values Survey,* the *Arab Barometer* and the PEW *Institute in Washington* (see below).

6.2 Open Society and Political Islam

The results of our study on *political Islam* in the Arab world certainly also have some very shocking aspects that cannot simply be swept under the carpet. Weighted by population, the *Arab Barometer* data show that more than 70% of Arabs have a (sympathetic) understanding of the anti-American terror that culminated in 9/11 in Manhattan. More than 44% of Arabs favour Sharia with corporal punishment, more than 37% want the rights of non-Muslims in society to be less than those of Muslims, and more than 34% also want Sharia to restrict the rights of women (Fig. 6.1).

Electronic Appendix Table 13 provides an *informed estimate of* actual, realistic data on imminent immigration from the Arab world to the two EU core states of France and Germany. Interested readers will find the rationale for our *cautious estimates* in the footnotes to the table.

There are not millions who will come to Germany and France with an imprint of *political Islam,* but the numbers in the upper six figures give pause for thought.

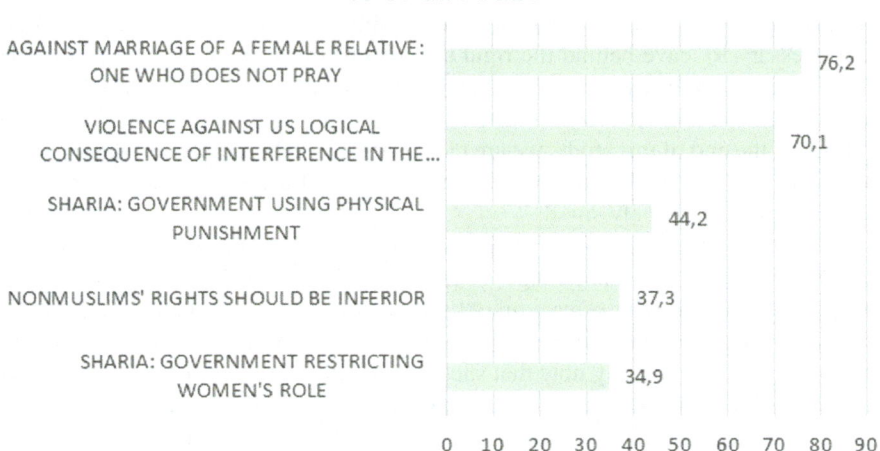

Fig. 6.1 Sharia with corporal punishment in Europe? The Herculean task of changing values in the Arab world—population-weighted shares of the total Arab population that clearly support Islamist positions according to the Arab *Barometer* data

6.3 For an Integration Policy Based on Trust in the Spirit of Harvard Professor Alberto Alesina (1957–2020)

In our study, many results were obtained, probably surprising for most, which show very openly what still needs to be done with regard to Islamist radicalism, but the author of this study does not want to conclude his text without also addressing an optimistic aspect which will mean an important field of work for the future for the work of religious communities in Europe and the rest of the West. If one follows Harvard economist Alberto Alesina, it is clear that trust in society as a whole and trust in individual institutions are essential factors of production. With Hichem Karoui, I wrote the book "*Les Musulmans: un cauchemar ou une force pour l'Europe?*" for the Paris publishing house *L'Harmattan* in 2011, and even then, we raised the question of the integration surpluses and deficits that can undoubtedly be derived from the international data on Muslims in Europe. Ten years later, I return to this question. Data from other European states point in the same direction; here it is permissible to analyse Austrian data in our freely available data appendix for the time being (https://www.academia.edu/79716351/Electronic_Appendix_Political_Islam_and_Religiously_Motivated_Political_Extremism_An_International_Comparison). There is Muslim trust in our institutions in Austria in many areas of society, and it is important to build on this trust politically in the coming years after the COVID-19 pandemic.

Our study has thus briefly shown some of the challenges but also optimistic perspectives of hope associated with the topic. We refer, as earlier, to the perspectives established in Solomon (2016), Solomon and Tausch (2020a, 2020b, 2021a,

2021b), and clearly establish here, first, that there are wide gradations of support for political Islam in the Arab world, second, that—true to the research of Falco and Rotondi (2016a, 2016b)—support for political Islam among the population groups ready to migrate is lower than among the population as a whole, but that the integration tasks in the migration recipient countries will continue to be very great, also and especially with regard to the acceptance of changed gender roles and religious tolerance. Thirdly, we must also note that the rejection of political violence in broad sectors of the population in Muslim countries gives cause for hope for the future, as does the trust in the institutions of state security expressed by Muslim populations across Western countries today. One of the most surprising aspects of our research for the political debate in Western Europe is that it is not the Arab region, and certainly not the Arab region as a whole, that is to be identified with the acceptance of political violence, while Southeast Asia as well as Iraq and Spain, on the other hand, are real problem zones. The real problem cases of religiously motivated political extremism are Tajikistan, Philippines, Vietnam, South Korea, Malaysia, Iraq, Macau SAR, Lebanon, Slovakia, Hong Kong SAR, Thailand, Bangladesh, Mexico, Chile, Ukraine, Russia, Bolivia, Ecuador, Spain, Kazakhstan, Lithuania, Guatemala, Nigeria and Indonesia. Given the great trust that Muslim populations in the West have in the institutions of state security, it would be worth trying to promote existing approaches to the integration of Muslims into the security apparatuses, such as the police, the military, the judiciary, and to promote targeted integration programmes into the civil service in general.

Open Access This chapter is licensed under the terms of the Creative Commons Attribution 4.0 International License (http://creativecommons.org/licenses/by/4.0/), which permits use, sharing, adaptation, distribution and reproduction in any medium or format, as long as you give appropriate credit to the original author(s) and the source, provide a link to the Creative Commons license and indicate if changes were made.

The images or other third party material in this chapter are included in the chapter's Creative Commons license, unless indicated otherwise in a credit line to the material. If material is not included in the chapter's Creative Commons license and your intended use is not permitted by statutory regulation or exceeds the permitted use, you will need to obtain permission directly from the copyright holder.

Literature Used and Further Reading

Achilov, D. (2016). Revisiting *Political Islam*: Explaining the nexus between *Political Islam* and contentious politics in the Arab World. *Social Science Quarterly, 97*(2), 252–270.

Akbarzadeh, S. (Ed.). (2020). *Routledge handbook of political Islam*. Routledge.

Alesina, A., & Giuliano, P. (2015). Culture and institutions. *Journal of Economic Literature, 53*(4), 898–944.

Alesina, A., Algan, Y., Cahuc, P., & Giuliano, P. (2015). Family values and the regulation of labour. *Journal of the European Economic Association, 13*(4), 599–630.

Almond, G. A., & Verba, S. (1963). *The civic culture: Political attitudes and democracy in five nations*. Princeton University Press.

Arab Opinion Index. (2015). *Arab public opinion programme (Arab center for research and policy studies)*. Doha, Qatar. http://english.dohainstitute.org/file/Get/6ad332dc-b805-4941-8a30-4d28806377c4. Accessed 10 May 2017.

Arena, M. D. C. P. (2017). Changing foreign policy: The Obama Administration's decision to oust Mubarak. *Revista Brasileira de Política Internacional, 60*. Available at: https://www.scielo.br/j/rbpi/a/k6bDGPqN8NWYsRbxVTmv47n/?lang=en.

Barro, R. J. (2003a). Economic growth in a cross section of countries. *International Library of Critical Writings in Economics, 159*(1), 350–386.

Barro, R. J. (2003b). *Religion adherence data*. Harvard University, Department of Economics. https://scholar.harvard.edu/Barro/publications/religion-adherence-data.

Basilevsky, A. T. (2009). *Statistical factor analysis and related methods: Theory and applications* (Vol. 418). John Wiley & Sons.

Baswedan, A. R. (2004). *Political Islam* in Indonesia: Present and future trajectory. *Asian Survey, 44*(5), 669–690.

Blalock, H. M. (1972). *Social statistics*. McGraw-Hill.

Blaydes, L. & Linzer, D. A. (2010). *Losing Muslim Hearts and Minds: Religiosity, Elite Competition, and Anti-Americanism in the Islamic World*. Available at http://web.stanford.edu/~blaydes/AA_ISA.pdf.

Blaydes, L., & Linzer D. A. (2012). Elite competition, religiosity, and anti-Americanism in the Islamic world. *American Political Science Review, 106*(02), 225–243.

Braithwaite, V. A., & Law, H. G. (1985). Structure of human values: Testing the adequacy of the Rokeach value survey. *Journal of Personality and Social Psychology, 49*(1), 250.

Brenner, P. S. (2016). Cross-national trends in religious service attendance. *Public Opinion Quarterly*, nfw016.

Browne, M. W. (2001). An overview of analytic rotation in exploratory factor analysis. *Multivariate Behavioral Research, 36*(1), 111–150.

© The Author(s) 2023
A. Tausch, *Political Islam and Religiously Motivated Political Extremism*,
SpringerBriefs in Political Science,
https://doi.org/10.1007/978-3-031-24854-2

Burgat, F. (2019). *Understanding political Islam*. Manchester University Press.
Cammett, M. (1999). Defensive integration and late developers: The Gulf Cooperation Council and the Arab Maghreb Union. *Global Governance a Review of Multilateralism and International Organizations, 5*(3), 379–402.
Cammett, M. (2014). Is there an Islamist political advantage? *Annual Review of Political Science, 17*, 187–206.
Cammett, M. (2017). Development and underdevelopment in the Middle East and North Africa. In C. Lancaster & N. van de Walle (Eds.), *The Oxford Handbook of the Politics of Development*. Political Economy Online Publication Date: Jan 2017. https://doi.org/10.1093/oxfordhb/978019 9845156.013.25.
Cammett, M. (2018). Popular grievances in the Arab region: Evaluating explanations for discontent in the lead-up to the uprisings. *Middle East Development Journal, 10*(1), 64–96.
Cammett, M., Diwan, I., & Vartanova, I. (2020). Insecurity and political values in the Arab world. *Democratization, 27*(5), 699–716. https://doi.org/10.1080/13510347.2020.1723081.
Cammett, M., et al. (2015). *A political economy of the middle east* (4th ed.). Boulder, CO: Westview Press.
Carnap, R. (1988). *Meaning and necessity: a study in semantics and modal logic* (Vol. 30). University of Chicago Press.
Cattell, R. (Ed.). (2012). *The scientific use of factor analysis in behavioural and life sciences*. Springer Science & Business Media.
Cesari, J. (2018). *What is political Islam?* Lynne Rienner Publishers.
Cesari, J. (2021). *Political Islam*: More than Islamism. *Religions, 12*(5), 299. Available at: https://doi.org/10.3390/rel12050299 and https://www.mdpi.com/2077-1444/12/5/299/htm.
Ciftci, S. (2010). Modernization, Islam, or social capital: What explains attitudes towards democracy in the Muslim world? *Comparative Political Studies, 43*(11), 1442–1470.
Ciftci, S. (2012). Islamophobia and threat perceptions: Explaining anti-Muslim sentiment in the West. *Journal of Muslim Minority Affairs, 32*(3), 293–309. https://doi.org/10.1080/13602004. 2012.727291.
Ciftci, S. (2013). Secular-Islamist cleavage, values, and support for democracy and Shari'a in the Arab World (December 26, 2012). *Political Research Quarterly, 66*(4), 781–793. Available at SSRN: https://ssrn.com/abstract=2920382.
Clauß, G., & Ebner, H. (1970). *Fundamentals of statistics for psychologists, pedagogues and sociologists*. Volk und Wissen Volkseigener Verlag.
Cornell University Roper Center. (2017). *Polling fundamentals—total survey error*. https://ropercenter.cornell.edu/support/polling-fundamentals-total-survey-error/. Accessed 22 May 2021.
Davidov, E., Schmidt, P., & Schwartz, S. H. (2008). Bringing values back in: The adequacy of the European social survey to measure values in 20 countries. *Public Opinion Quarterly, 72*(3), 420–445.
de Soysa, I., & Nordås, R. (2007). Islam's bloody innards? Religion and political terror, 1980–2000. *International Studies Quarterly, 51*(4), 927–943.
Driessen, M. D. (2014). *Religion and democratization: Framing religious and political identities in Muslim and Catholic societies*. Oxford University Press.
Driessen, M. D. (2018). Sources of Muslim democracy: The supply and demand of religious policies in the Muslim world. *Democratization, 25*(1), 115–135. https://doi.org/10.1080/13510347.2017. 1334054.
Esposito, J. (2012). *Political Islam and the West*. https://www.researchgate.net/publication/235214 754_Political_Islam_and_the_West.
Fabrigar, L. R., Wegener, D. T., MacCallum, R. C., & Strahan, E. J. (1999). Evaluating the use of exploratory factor analysis in psychological research. *Psychological Methods, 4*(3), 272.
Falco, C., & Rotondi, V. (2016a). *Political Islam*, internet use and willingness to migrate: Evidence from the *Arab Barometer*. *Peace Economics, Peace Science and Public Policy, 22*(1), 73–95. https://doi.org/10.1515/peps-2015-0045.

Falco, C., & Rotondi, V. (2016b). The less extreme, the more you leave: Radical Islam and willingness to migrate. *World Development, 88*, 122–133. https://doi.org/10.1016/j.worlddev.2016.07.017.

Faßmann, H., & Hintermann, C. (1997). *Migration potential East Central Europe: Structure and motivation of potential migrants from Poland, Slovakia, the Czech Republic and Hungary*. Verlag der Österreichischen Akademie der Wissenschaften.

Faßmann, H., & Münz, R. (1994). European east-west migration, 1945–1992. *International Migration Review, 28*(3), 520–538.

Finch, H. (2006). Comparison of the performance of varimax and promax rotations: Factor structure recovery for dichotomous items. *Journal of Educational Measurement, 43*(1), 39–52.

Fleischmann, F., Phalet, K., & Klein, O. (2011). Religious identification and politicization in the face of discrimination: Support for *Political Islam* and political action among the Turkish and Moroccan second generation in Europe. *British Journal of Social Psychology, 50*(4), 628–648.

Fox, A. M., Abdelkarim Alzwawi, S., & Refki, D. (2016). Islamism, secularism and the woman question in the aftermath of the Arab spring: Evidence from the *Arab Barometer*. *Politics and Governance, 4*(4), 40–57.

Fox, J. (2019). *The correlates of religion and state*. Routledge.

Fox, J. (2000). *A world survey of religion and the state*. Cambridge University Press.

Fox, J., & Akbaba, Y. (2015). Securitization of Islam and religious discrimination: Religious minorities in Western democracies, 1990–2008. *Comparative European Politics, 13*(2), 175–197.

Fox, J., Sandler, S., & Sandier, S. (2004). *Bringing religion into international relations* (pp. 9–10). New York: Palgrave Macmillan.

Gorsuch, R. L. (1983). *Factor analysis*. Erlbaum.

Gülalp, H. (2001). Globalisation and *political Islam*: The social bases of Turkey's welfare party. *International Journal of Middle East Studies, 33*(3), 433–448.

Gumuscu, S. (2010). Class, status, and party: The changing face of *Political Islam* in Turkey and Egypt. *Comparative Political Studies, 43*(7), 835–861.

Haerpfer, C., Inglehart, R., Moreno, A., Welzel, Kizilova, Diez-Medrano, J., Lagos, M., Norris, P., Ponarin, E., & Puranen, B., et al. (Eds.). (2020). *World Values Survey: Round seven-country-pooled datafile*. JD Systems Institute & WVSA Secretariat. https://doi.org/10.14281/18241.1..

Hafez, F. (2014). *Islamic political thinkers: An introduction to the Islamic political history of ideas*. Peter Lang GmbH, Internationaler Verlag der Wissenschaften.

Harman, H. H. (1976). *Modern factor analysis* (3rd ed.). University of Chicago Press.

Hashemi, N. (2021). *Political Islam*: A 40 year retrospective. *Religions, 12*(2), 130. https://doi.org/10.3390/rel12020130.

Hedges, L. V., & Olkin, I. (2014). *Statistical methods for meta-analysis*. Academic press.

Henne, P. S. (2012). The two swords: Religion-state connections and interstate disputes. *Journal of Peace Research, 49*, 153–768.

Inglehart, R. F. (1988). The renaissance of political culture. *American Political Science Review, 82*(04), 1203–1230.

Inglehart, R. F. (2006). Mapping global values. *Comparative Sociology, 5*(2), 115–136.

Inglehart, R. F. (2018). *Cultural Evolution: People's Motivations are Changing, and Reshaping the World*. Cambridge, U.K.: Cambridge University Press.

Inglehart, R. F., & Baker, W. E. (2000). Modernization, cultural change, and the persistence of traditional values. *American Sociological Review, 65*(1), 19–51. Available at: http://scholar.google.at/citations?view_op=view_citation&hl=de&user=r3vC6IAAAAAJ&citation_for_view=r3vC6IAAAAAJ:9yKSN-GCB0IC.

Inglehart, R. F., & Norris, P. (2003a). *Rising tide: Gender equality and cultural change around the world*. Cambridge University Press.

Inglehart, R. F., & Norris, P. (2003b). The true clash of civilizations. *Foreign Policy*, 63–70.

Inglehart, R. F., & Norris, P. (2012). The four horsemen of the apocalypse: Understanding human security. *Scandinavian Political Studies, 35*(1), 71–95.

Inglehart, R. F., & Norris, P. (2016). *Trump, brexit, and the rise of populism: Economic have-nots and cultural backlash*. Available at SSRN: http://ssrn.com/abstract=2818659. HKS Working Paper No. RWP16-026.

Inglehart, R. F., & Welzel, C. (2003). Political culture and democracy: Analyzing cross-level linkages. *Comparative Politics, 36*(1), 61–79.

Inglehart, R. F., & Welzel, C. (2009, March, April). How development leads to democracy. What we know about modernization. *Foreign Affairs*. http://www.foreignaffairs.com/articles/64821/ronald-Inglehart-and-christian-welzel/how-development-leads-to-democracy.

INSS (Institute for National Security Studies, Tel Aviv. (2020). *Strategic survey for Israel 2019–2020*. Available at https://www.INSS.org.il/publication/strategic-survey-for-israel-2019-2020/.

Kim, S. Y. (2010). Do Asian values exist? Empirical tests of the four dimensions of Asian values. *Journal of East Asian Studies*, 315–344.

Kline, P. (2014). *An easy guide to factor analysis*. Routledge.

Knippenberg, H. (2015). Secularization and transformation of religion in post-war Europe. In *The changing world religion appendix map* (pp. 2101–2127). Springer Netherlands.

Kucinskas, J., & Van Der Does, T. (2017). Gender ideals in turbulent times: An examination of insecurity, Islam, and Muslim men's gender attitudes during the Arab Spring. *Comparative Sociology, 16*(3), 340–368. https://doi.org/10.1163/15691330-12341428.

Kuznets, S. (1940). Schumpeter's Business Cycles. *American Economic Review, 30*(2), 157–169.

Kuznets, S. (1955). Economic Growth and Income Inequality. *American Economic Review, 45*(1), 1–28.

Kuznets, S. (1976). *Modern Economic Growth: Rate, Structure and Spread*. New Haven, CT: Yale University Press.

Langer Research Associates. (n.d.). Moe. http://www.langerresearch.com/moe/. Accessed 23 May 2021.

McCleary, R. M., & Barro, R. J. (2006a). Religion and economy. *The Journal of Economic Perspectives, 20*(2), 49–72.

McCleary, R. M., & Barro, R. J. (2006b). Religion and political economy in an international panel. *Journal for the Scientific Study of Religion, 45*(2), 149–175.

McDonald, R. P. (2014). *Factor analysis and related methods*. Psychology Press.

Mecham, R. Q. (2004). From the ashes of virtue, a promise of light: The transformation of *Political Islam* in Turkey. *Third World Quarterly, 25*(2), 339–358.

Minkov, M. (2014). The K factor, societal hypometropia, and national values: A study of 71 nations. *Personality and Individual Differences, 66*, 153–159.

Minkov, M., & Hofstede, G. (2011). *Cultural differences in a globalizing world*. Emerald.

Minkov, M., & Hofstede, G. (2013). *Cross-cultural analysis: The science and art of comparing the world's modern societies and their cultures*. Sage.

Morel, J. S. J. (2003). *Radical church reform: For a courageous renewal: Facts and sociological theories of religion on the crisis of the Catholic Church from 1950 to the present as a basis for decisions on necessary reforms*. Tyrolia-Verlag.

Mulaik, S. A. (2009). *Foundations of factor analysis*. CRC Press.

Noman, A. (Ed.). (2012). *Good growth and governance in Africa: Rethinking development strategies*. Oxford University Press.

Norris, P., & Inglehart, R. F. (2012). Muslim integration into Western cultures: Between origins and destinations. *Political Studies, 60*(2), 228–251.

Norris, P., & Inglehart, R. F. (2015). Are high levels of existential security conducive to secularization? A response to our critics. In *The changing world religion map* (pp. 3389–3408). Springer Netherlands.

Olson, M. (1982). *The rise and decline of nations: Economic growth, stagflation, and social rigidities*. Yale University Press.

Öniş, Z. (2001). *Political Islam* at the crossroads: From hegemony to co-existence. *Contemporary Politics, 7*(4), 281–298.

Özbudun, E. (2006). From *Political Islam* to conservative democracy: The case of the justice and development party in Turkey. *South European Society and Politics, 11*(3–4), 543–557.

Rahbarqazi, M., & Mahmoudoghli, R. (2020). Corruption perceptions, political distrust, and the weakening of political Islam in Iraq [Percepciones de la corrupción, desconfianza política, y el debilitamiento del Islam político en Irak]. *Revista Espanola De Sociologia, 29*(3), 57–74. https://doi.org/10.22325/FES/RES.2020.57.

Rummel, R. J. (1970). *Applied factor analysis*. Northwestern University Press.

Silver, B. D., & Dowley, K. M. (2000). Measuring political culture in multiethnic societies reaggregating the *World Values Survey*. *Comparative Political Studies, 33*(4), 517–550.

Solomon, H. (2016). *Islamic State and the coming global confrontation*. Springer.

Solomon, H., & Tausch, A. (2020a). *Islamism, crisis and democratization: Implications of the World Values Survey for the Muslim World. (Perspectives on development in the Middle East and North Africa (Mena region))*. Springer.

Solomon, H., & Tausch, A. (2020b). The demise of the Muslim brotherhood in the Arab World? *Jewish Political Studies Review, 31*(1/2), 171–209.

Solomon, H., & Tausch, A. (2021a) *Political Islam* in the Arab MENA countries: The evidence from the *Arab Barometer* (5) Data About the "Unword" of Middle East research? In *Arab MENA countries: Vulnerabilities and constraints against democracy on the eve of the Global COVID-19 crisis. Perspectives on Development in the Middle East and North Africa (MENA) Region*. Springer. https://doi.org/10.1007/978-981-15-7047-6_7.

Solomon, H., & Tausch, A. (2021b). *Arab MENA countries: Vulnerabilities and constraints against democracy on the eve of the global Covid-19 crisis. (Perspectives on development in the Middle East and North Africa (Mena region)*. Springer.

Suhr, D. (2012). Exploratory factor analysis with the *World Values Survey*. In *Proceedings of the SAS Global Forum 2012 Conference*. Orlando, FL.

Tausch, A. (2010a). *Armut und Radikalität?: Soziologische Perspektiven zur Integration der Muslim*innen in Europa basierend auf dem "World Values Survey und dem "European Social Survey")* (1st ed.) (Studies in comparative social pedagogy and international social work and social policy, 12). Europäischer Hochschulverlag.

Tausch, A. (2010b). Globalization and development: The relevance of classical "dependency" theory for the world today. *International Social Science Journal, 61*(202), 467–488.

Tausch, A. (2010c). Paul Boccara's analysis of global capitalism. The return of the Bourbons, and the breakdown of the Brussels/Paris neo-liberal consensus. *Entelequia. Revista Interdisciplinar, 12*, 105–147.

Tausch, A. (2016a). Is globalization really good for public health? *The International Journal of Health Planning and Management, 31*(4), 511–536.

Tausch, A. (2016b). Islamism and Antisemitism. Preliminary evidence on their relationship from cross-national opinion data. *Social Evolution & History, 15*(2), 50–99 (Uchitel Publishing House, Moscow), and *Journal of Globalization Studies, 7*(2), 137–170 (Uchitel Publishing House, Moscow).

Tausch, A. (2016c). Muslim immigration continues to divide Europe: A quantitative analysis of European social survey data. *Middle East Review of International Affairs, 20*(2).

Tausch, A. (2016d, April). *The civic culture of the Arab World: A comparative analysis based on World Values Survey data*. Middle East Review of International Affairs, Rubin Center, Research in International Affairs, IDC Herzliya, Israel. Available at: SSRN: https://ssrn.com/abstract=2827232 or https://doi.org/10.2139/ssrn.2827232.

Tausch, A. (2019a). Migration from the Muslim world to the West: Its most recent trends and effects. *Jewish Political Studies Review, 30*(1–2), 65–225. Available at http://jcpa.org/article/migration-from-the-muslim-world-to-the-west-its-most-recent-trends-and-effects/ (with data definitions and sources). Free data download available from https://www.academia.edu/37568941/Migration_from_the_Muslim_World_to_the_West_Its_Most_Recent_Trends_and_Effects.

Tausch, A. (2019b). Multivariate analyses of the global acceptability rates of male intimate partner violence (IPV) against women based on *World Values Survey* data. *International Journal of Health Planning and Management*. https://doi.org/10.1002/hpm.2781.

Tausch, A. (2019c). Muslim integration or alienation in non-Muslim-majority countries. *Jewish Political Studies Review, 30*(3/4), 55–99.

Tausch, A. (2021a). *Islamism. Global surveys and implications for the future of the Arab countries*. Nova Science Publishers.

Tausch, A. (2021b, September). Islamist terrorism, *Political Islam* and migration in Western Europe. In H. Solomon (Ed.), *Directions in international terrorism. Theories, trends and trajectories*. Palgrave Macmillan, ISBN 978-981-16-3379-9.

Tausch, A. (2021c, September). Social attitudes fueling Islamist terrorism. In H. Solomon (Ed.), *Directions in international terrorism. Theories, trends and trajectories*. Palgrave Macmillan, ISBN 978-981-16-3379-9.

Tausch, A., & Heshmati, A. (2013). *Globalization, the human condition, and sustainable development in the twenty-first century: Cross-national perspectives and European implications*. Anthem Press (with data definitions and sources). Free data download available from https://www.academia.edu/35044095/Globalization_the_human_condition_and_sustainable_development_in_the_21st_Century._Cross-national_perspectives_and_European_implications_Cod ebook_and_EXCEL_data_file.

Tausch, A., Heshmati, A., & Karoui, H. (2014). *The political algebra of global value change: General models and implications for the Muslim world*. Nova Science Publishers.

Tausch, A., & Karoui, H. (2011). *Les Musulmans: Un cauchemar ou une force pour l'Europe?* Editions L'Harmattan.

Tausch, A., & Moaddel, M. (2009). *What 1.3 billion Muslims really think. An answer to a recent Gallup study, based on the 'World Values Survey'*. Nova Science Publishers.

Tausch, A., & Prager, F. (1993). *Towards a Socio-Liberal Theory of World Development*. Basingstoke and New York: Palgrave Macmillan/St. Martins Press.

Taylor, M., & Elbushra, M. E. (2006). Research note: Hassan al-Turabi, Osama bin Laden, and Al Qaeda in Sudan. *Terrorism and Political Violence, 18*(3), 449–464. https://doi.org/10.1080/09546550600752022.

Tessler, M. (2010). Religion, religiosity and the place of Islam in political life: Insights from the Arab barometer surveys. *Middle East Law and Governance, 2*(2), 221–252. https://doi.org/10.1163/187633710X500748.

Volpi, F. (2011). *Political Islam: A critical reader*. Routledge.

Wegner, E., & Cavatorta, F. (2019). Revisiting the Islamist-secular divide: Parties and voters in the Arab world. *International Political Science Review, 40*(4), 558–575. https://doi.org/10.1177/0192512118784225.

Yeşilada, B. A., & Noordijk, P. (2010). Changing values in Turkey: Religiosity and tolerance in comparative perspective. *Turkish Studies, 11*(1), 9–27.

Zak, P. J., & Knack, S. (2001). Trust and growth. *The Economic Journal, 111*(470), 295–321.

The manufacturer's authorised representative in the EU is Springer Nature Customer Service Centre GmbH, Europaplatz 3, 69115 Heidelberg, Germany. If you have any concerns regarding our products, please contact ProductSafety@springernature.com

Printed and bound by CPI Group (UK) Ltd, Croydon, CR0 4YY
25/03/2026
02078170-0009